MISSION: CAREER TRANSITION

A CAREER CHANGE GUIDE FOR INTELLIGENCE,
MILITARY, FOREIGN AFFAIRS, NATIONAL
SECURITY, AND OTHER GOVERNMENT
PROFESSIONALS

ALISON PENTZ BOUWMEESTER

With a Foreword by
THE HONORABLE SUSAN M. GORDON
Former Principal Deputy Director of National Intelligence

. . .

APB Books

Publisher: APB BOOKS

Reston, Virginia 20191

ISBN- 978-1-7351267-0-8

First Edition 2020

Manufactured in the United States of America

For information regarding special discounts for bulk purchases, please contact: *admin@futurityservices.com.*

DEDICATION

Paul H. Bouwmeester

This book is dedicated to my husband of 30 years, Paul H. Bouwmeester, who "transitioned" jobs, locations, and employers with me dozens of times since we were married in 1990. He helped me keep my priorities through it all. He also contributed valuable content and wisdom to Chapter 5 and authored Chapter 13 of this book as an experienced Human Resources Senior Executive in private industry.

Government spouses and partners are critical members of our national security team because they are the cornerstone of our individual support systems. Paul was the glue that held our family together, and without him, I would have been lost. Being the "trailing spouse" of an intelligence officer is not for the faint of heart. Being the foreign-born spouse of a female U.S. intelligence officer requires even more courage, especially considering stereotypes, assumptions, and some truly unique challenges. Paul handled all these situations with humor and dignity (being followed and listened to and videotaped by foreign intelligence services, for example). His untiring dedication to support my career, our family, our Agency mission and our national security cannot be understated. He was unwavering, even in those times when many other Agency spouses decided that this chaotic life was not for them.

Paul did all of this for me and us while also having a noteworthy professional career of his own, culminating in an eight-year run as Global Vice President for Human Resources for an international IT services company. This book benefits from Paul's professional expertise in finance, corporate recruitment, and contract offer negotiations, as well as helping readers understand their corporate compensation and benefits options. Thank you, and well done, Paul!

Paul and I are fortunate to have two amazing adult sons. Our boys benefitted from an upbringing in very interesting places around the world. Life as "Agency brats" gave them global perspective, an understanding of the importance of diversity, and an appreciation for world cultures. They are engaged, responsible citizens. We are very proud of them both, not only for their individual accomplishments as young men, but also for taking my own oath seriously and carefully "keeping the secret" about where Mom really worked for so many years. I am truly grateful for their maturity, discretion, and humor. I loved our worldly adventures together!

Alison Pentz Bouwmeester

FOREWORD

BY THE HONORABLE SUSAN M. GORDON,
Former Principal Deputy Director of National Intelligence

Who wouldn't want sage counsel from a career clandestine operative used to making impossible, impactful decisions of consequence, under the most trying of circumstances, when there are more unknowns than knowns, and who lived to tell about each of them?

Of course, no one.

Especially when making the most personal, impactful, consequential decision of any adult's life—deciding what to do after you've done what you started out to do; and in the case of a career public servant, after you've been so singularly focused on mission you simply forgot that one day you would move on, and you're surprised to find yourself here.

That's why you picked up this book and are reading it.

You've taken the first step. You've recognized the moment in which you find yourself—knowing that there surely is wisdom of others that you can use when transitioning from a world you know to a world you've largely ignored, and choosing a Sherpa who has the experience, credibility, and (yes) sources to be worthy of your time and decision.

I first met the author in the winter of 2010 when I interviewed her for a leadership position in my organization. I didn't offer Alison the job—and no, not because I am a Dukie and she was a Tarheel in spy's clothing; I don't care what she says. I didn't offer her the job because it wasn't the right job for her, nor she for it. When I told her of my decision, I also said I would make it my mission to work with her one day, because I thought she was special—more courageous, more honest, more capable, and more straightforward than many of the also remarkable officers with whom I had worked at the Central Intelligence Agency (CIA). Two months later, I fulfilled that mission of getting her to work with me—to my great honor, joy, and lasting effect on my life.

Alison and I were both career intelligence officers, although for the better part of our careers we never crossed paths. My career was almost exclusively domestic, disproportionately in science and technology, and for all but six of my more than 30 years, as a leader of successively large organizations. Hers was based in the foreign field, conducting human operations, and though she surely led, it was more as player-coach than straight line manager. What immediately leapt off the page at me when we met was her remarkable combination of steely-eyed focus, imperturbable calm, orderly mind, and intrinsic humanity. Even more, this was someone who understood how to process uncertainty, how to manage risk, and how to find a way forward.

I remember Alison's retirement ceremony like it was a minute ago. Packed room, the delightful poignance of shared memories, the heartfelt tributes for a job well done, and the duality of excitement for and trepidation of what lay ahead. We hugged her goodbye, showed her the door, and wished her "good luck" with her next adventure…whatever the heck *that* was going to be. And then I watched as she got her first new job, then her second, won tennis championships, raised funds to fight breast cancer, formed her own company, celebrated milestones in her sons' lives, gave back to our Agency, and, most recently, wrote this book—answering for all of us the questions that had hung in the air when she left the work life she had known that day, nine years before.

What sets this book apart to me is threefold: It is focused on the particular circumstance of career national security professionals who are leaving their first jobs after 20-40 years of consuming dedication; it breaks down a complex blob (technical term) of career transition issues (why, when, what, and how) into manageable bits with a roadmap of how to navigate each; and by presenting combined wisdom of not only Alison, but tens of colleagues who have traveled the same path as you in gritty, candid detail. You will see yourself (and your circumstance, and your fears, and your hopes and dreams) in these pages. And you will know that you're not alone, you're not weird, and there is as great a future ahead as there was a past.

I wish Alison had written this book sooner or that I had left government service later. I've found my way, but it would have been easier with Alison and her mates' wisdom in my head and toolkit in my hands. Whether you prefer the philosophical or the dispassionately practical when problem solving; whether you're making your first post-Federal transition or your nth; and whether you want to continue to be who you were or become who you will be, this book will help you on your way.

Trust me, I used to be from the government.

Susan M. Gordon
Former Principal Deputy Director of National Intelligence

CONTENTS

PART I

1

INTRODUCTION

My Career Made a Difference to Our National Security: So Now What?

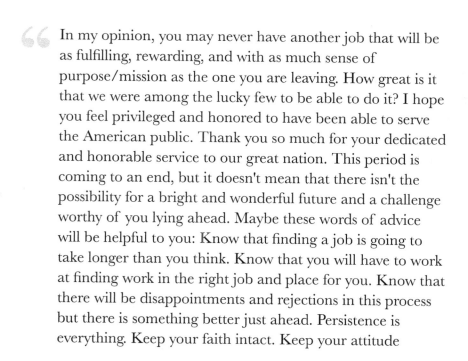 In my opinion, you may never have another job that will be as fulfilling, rewarding, and with as much sense of purpose/mission as the one you are leaving. How great is it that we were among the lucky few to be able to do it? I hope you feel privileged and honored to have been able to serve the American public. Thank you so much for your dedicated and honorable service to our great nation. This period is coming to an end, but it doesn't mean that there isn't the possibility for a bright and wonderful future and a challenge worthy of you lying ahead. Maybe these words of advice will be helpful to you: Know that finding a job is going to take longer than you think. Know that you will have to work at finding work in the right job and place for you. Know that there will be disappointments and rejections in this process but there is something better just ahead. Persistence is everything. Keep your faith intact. Keep your attitude

positive and self-esteem healthy. Keep your loved ones close, take care of them, and rely on your friends and family for support...they are in this with you. There is a great and wonderful life ahead, full of new things to learn and experiences to be had. There are rewards in this 'next chapter' and they can be incredible. My very best wishes for 'the hunt' and I hope that your next career provides you with the ability to live the life of your dreams.

(Anonymous Interview Subject, FBI)

This book was written to help Intelligence, Foreign Affairs, Military, National Security and other government professionals approach the daunting task of leaving their current government service. It was primarily written for those in the Federal Government community who are considering retirement, but it also contains information of value to those leaving government short of a full career. When I left the Central Intelligence Agency (CIA), there was no "handbook" for those who were considering separation from government service. I wished that there had been one — hence this book.

I dreaded leaving the CIA ("the Agency"), which had been my tribe since the year that I graduated from college. It was a family of amazing, intelligent people with a shared mission that we all took very seriously. It was hard to imagine leaving a place where I believed that my work really mattered to our national security. How could anything replace this incredible life? How would I fill the time? What would make me feel fulfilled?

During the last year of my Agency career, I hired an Executive Coach, Roger Campbell, an Agency retiree who had himself successfully transitioned. I had hoped that Roger would tell me when it was finally time to retire. But he would not and could not. Roger wisely knew that I needed to make (and to own) this important decision myself. Roger did help me evaluate the state of my career, my work and life priorities, and to consider the range of possibilities by asking hard questions and making me look inside myself. He was also extremely helpful when it was time to evaluate the terms of specific job offers that came my way, coaching me for interviews, and guiding me to negotiate contract terms that were most beneficial to me. Thank you, Roger. You influenced me in many ways and continue to be a mentor in my own new path in coaching others.

The ease with which I transitioned from government was due, in part, to the outstanding Career Transition Program and Horizons course at the CIA. It is probably the best program in government for helping employees to consider the whole range of topics that are part of life and career transitions. I also received very valuable guidance and advice from many former colleagues who were extremely generous with their time, and who had, themselves, made successful transitions before me. Therefore, this guide also includes the guidance and sage wisdom of more than 30 former government professionals from the CIA, the National Security Agency (NSA), the Federal Bureau of Investigation (FBI), the U.S. Department of State (State Department), the National Geospatial Agency (NGA), the Office of the Director of National Intelligence (ODNI), the U.S. Military, and the U.S. Department of Treasury. I am very grateful to this group of Interview Subjects for candidly sharing their own transition experiences for the benefit of you, the readers.

HOW TO USE THIS BOOK

This Career Transition Guide is organized according the phases that are typically part of a career transition. There are generally three key elements to a separation from government:

1. The decision to leave (when to go and why)
2. Potential paths to consider (from jumping straight into full retirement to pursuing full-time employment and various options in-between)
3. The mechanics of leaving, including developing a career

transition strategy, determining your value proposition, resumés, networking, LinkedIn, interviewing, and negotiating an employment agreement if you elect to pursue onward employment.

This book can be read straight-through from start to finish, or can it be read in phases as you evaluate where you are in the transition process. The guide also includes practical worksheets and exercises to help you evaluate yourself, where you've been, and where you are going. You will find most of these worksheets in the earlier stages of the book as you consider the Big Decision and what you might like to do next. Doing serious self-assessment up front will help you avoid tangents and mis-starts along paths that might not ultimately be the best fit for you.

Government professionals have spent their entire careers singularly focused on the mission. Thinking about YOU and what you want/need does not come naturally and may be uncomfortable. But it's time! The included worksheets provide a frame-work to help you to think about your personal level of ambition, your vision for the future, the legacy you would like to leave behind, your personal and professional goals, your workplace values, along with a range of questions to consider when evaluating an offer of employment.

If you are just beginning to consider the idea of separating from the Federal Government, Part 2 of this book is for you! It will help you begin to evaluate whether this is the right time for you to go, and provides key questions to ask yourself about your state of mind and the reasons for it. Part 2 provides useful context in which to view your government service going forward. This section is designed to help you focus on readying yourself to make a smooth exit, with useful worksheets on such topics as: evaluating your financial readiness, the decision to work or not to work, understanding your monthly family budget, and (if you decide to seek onward employment), how to project your future salary requirements. Also in Part 2, many who have gone before you candidly discuss the human factors that are involved in the decision to leave government and provide valuable lessons-learned from their own successful transitions.

If you are already leaning toward leaving, then Part 3 of the Guide is for you. It provides the framework for you to plan your departure, including such topics as: whether or not to take time off before starting a new job, how much time you might expect a job search to take, and how long people generally stay in their first job out of government. We evaluate the range of post-separation options available to you, including immediate retirement, part-time and/or full-time work, and consulting options, as well as questions to help you evaluate the capacity in which you might like to work. Worksheets 6-10 help you consider how ambitious you might like to be in your next step, building your vision for your future, thinking about the legacy you might like to leave behind, your personal and professional goals, and your values.

Part 4 of the book focuses upon the actual mechanics of leaving, particularly for those who choose to continue working in some capacity. We discuss the marketable skills that government professionals bring to the private sector, and talk about the importance of understanding your values and goals. Before you write a resumé, Part 4 helps readers consider what their value proposition might be to a prospective employer. We also discuss resumés and job applications, professional networking, the use of LinkedIn, interviewing strategies, and what sorts of benefits options you might want to consider in a job offer.

Read on for loads of great tips on career transition from the Federal Government!

2

INTRODUCING THE METHODOLOGY AND THE INTERVIEW SUBJECTS (THE HOW AND THE WHO)

THE HOW

It is highly unusual to hear Intelligence, National Security, Foreign Affairs, Military and other Federal Government professionals candidly discussing their careers (and life after government) as a collective. The 33 Interview Subjects quoted in this book volunteered to share their own transition experiences to help others face their upcoming separation from government. The interviews were conducted in Spring 2020 through the use of a comprehensive survey that was designed to ferret-out valuable personal transition stories, good and bad experiences, lessons learned, advice, guidance, and pitfalls to avoid. These collective stories are intended to fill an information gap to help others facing an upcoming career transition—something that had been lacking when we, ourselves, separated from service.

Many have gone before you and there is a wealth of valuable transition guidance, advice and support that can and should be used. You will be surprised how willing others are to answer questions and lend a helping hand.

. . .

In the body of this book, I have selected quotes from survey respondents, all former government employees, that best exemplify the most common answers and the trends observed in the survey data collected. It was not possible to provide all the survey responses in this book given the high volume of data collected. I made a commitment to those interviewed that their responses would remain non-attributable to any individual, out of appreciation for the high level of candor with which they responded to my (sometimes very personal) questions.

THE WHO

Dozens of former colleagues, friends, and contacts collaborated with me on this book. They represent 33 successfully transitioned government officials (19 Women and 14 Men) who served at the Central Intelligence Agency (CIA), National Security Agency (NSA), Federal Bureau of Investigation (FBI), U.S. Department of State (Foreign Service), U.S. Treasury, National Geospatial Agency (NGA), Office of the Director of National Intelligence (ODNI), Department of Energy (DOE), and the U.S. Military. Many of them served in multiple agencies during their careers. When leaving government, they ranged in rank from GS-14 equivalent to SES/SIS/Military Flag Rank, with most being in the GS-15 or SIS/SES ranks. They all left government service between 2009 and 2020. Most of them retired from government service rather than separating prior to retirement eligibility. The comments in this book therefore mainly represent the perspective of those retiring from government.

What came next for them? Some of the Interview Subjects went directly from full-time government employment to being fully retired (with no second career or subsequent employment). Others sought and found part-time or Independent Consultant opportunities. Still others went back to work full time, either in the defense contracting sector or in other industries. Of those who went back to work, some of our Interview Subjects are now CEOs or COOs of small or medium-sized companies, or lead risk assessment units for major U.S. corporations. Others are on corporate boards and have a portfolio of part-time projects to keep them busy and fulfilled. Others have returned to staff augmentation roles with their previous employer. Their post-retirement experiences are diverse and representative of the range of opportunities that could be available to you after leaving government service.

Most of the Interview Subjects are identified by name with brief biographies in Appendix A at the end of this book. A few respondents asked to remain anonymous. All graciously provided highly personal vignettes, stories, thoughts and lessons-learned to benefit the readers who are considering leaving government.

A breakdown of the 33 Interview Subjects' previous organizational affiliation (the agency or organization from which they departed government service) is provided here:

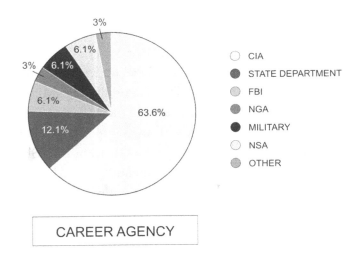

CAREER AGENCY

CIA (63.6%), State Department (12.1%), NSA (6.1%), Military (6.1%), FBI (6.1%), NGA (3.0%), Other (3.0%).

There was no obvious correlation that emerged between the organization from which someone separated and what they did next. (Keep in mind that the survey sample size was relatively small, and there are certainly additional next-step options available to those leaving government.) The paths listed here are only some of the potential options available.

Here were our Interview Subjects' chosen first steps after leaving government:

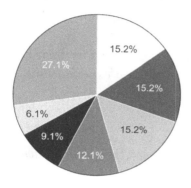

○ Sought full-time employment in a corporate capacity for a defense contractor or related industry
● Became self-employed
◐ Fully retired
◑ Sought full-time employment in an industry unrelated to your previous career
● Sought part-time employment
○ Sought full-time work doing staff augmentation in support of your previous employer
◐ Other (each 3 %)
   - Had pre-arranged executive position with a University FFRDC
   - Full-time employment in a private security firm supporting corporate clients
   - Sought full-time employment to give back to USG and capitalize on my unique leadership and experiences
   - Sought full-time work as a US government civilian for a different agency
   - Intended to seek some employment, but wanted to give myself time to explore
   - Sought full-time employment in an industry related to my previous career
   - Combination of seeking PT employment and becoming self-employed
   - Sought full-time employment at a nonprofit associated w/ the IC, DoD, & DHS
   - Taking time for elder care/child care; Advisory Board positions

How would you categorize your first step out of government?

In the pages ahead, our Interview Subjects discuss the decisions they made regarding their first steps out of government and the reasons they chose the paths they did. All say that post-government life is a happy place, although you will probably take several steps to find the best fit for yourself.

. . .

All the Interview Subjects want you to know that life outside of the Federal Government is full of positives and personal development. Of course, they all had fears. They still miss things from government service. They also note that you can (and will) find great personal and professional fulfillment in other things beyond your government career. The Interview Subjects also comment extensively in this book about how important it is to network with those who have left the Federal Government before you, and expressed their appreciation for those who mentored them in their own career transitions.

I am very grateful to these impressive men and women for their help with this project and for their willingness to share their experiences to benefit the reader.

Alison Pentz Bouwmeester

PART II

THE DECISION TO LEAVE
(WHEN TO GO AND WHY)

3

PERHAPS IT'S TIME TO GO. HOW DO I KNOW?

GETTING YOUR HEAD IN THE GAME

Deciding to leave a Military, Intelligence, Foreign Affairs, or National Security career, for whatever reason, could be the hardest decision you will ever make. On the emotional side, it can be scary, exciting, intimidating, liberating, thrilling, and depressing all at the same time. **It's normal to have all those conflicting feelings.** It is also human to second-guess your decision to resign/retire/separate. For many of us, it can be daunting to think about leaving a career where you spent 20–40 years working side-by side in challenging situations with amazing people in a very mission-focused profession. Some of us fought the Cold War and the ongoing War on Terror. We worked through the September 11 tragedy, the 2020 global pandemic, and handled many other major threats to our national security. Handing over your badge, taking off a uniform, walking out the door, and leaving dear friends and colleagues behind is no small decision.

You can avoid falling into the trap of lamenting a loss of the past. To ease your transition, try to shift into a forward-looking mindset. Frame your past government service as a stage in your life (like your educational years), and consider your newest hopes and goals as you look toward the future. If you are retiring from Federal Service, remind yourself that "you have had an amazing career". It was rewarding and fulfilling. Take great satisfaction in a job well done! Take pride in having served your country honorably and with distinction. Whatever comes next personally and professionally, try to place it in the broader context of your adult life. A "second career", whether paid or unpaid, can be an amazing opportunity to learn new skills, to remain intellectually challenged, to share your wisdom and experience, and to mentor and give back. It will require a recalibration for those who have grown accustomed to a highly-structured environment where rank and protocol are strictly adhered to, where creativity and thinking outside the box is not always valued/encouraged. Begin now to think about your vision and dreams for the future—before you separate. Start to put the connections and the infrastructure in place now. Ease your transition by planning ahead.

Look at Career Transition as an opportunity to learn new things, grow, give back, focus on your health, refresh relationships, travel, re-energize, and become whatever you wish to be.

 "It was the realization that I was no longer excited about the job opportunities being presented to me as I was wrapping up a two-year special project - and they were positions that I had long coveted. I was no longer inspired or excited about them."

Interview Subject, government retiree, on deciding to move on to a new challenge

MAKING THE BIG DECISION

People decide to transition out for a wide variety of reasons. Some go because they want to learn something new, they see no other opportunities for career advancement, or they have grown weary and cynical. Occasionally, colleagues leave because they feel wronged. Others leave because of philosophical differences with the administration or their organization, they have more pressing life priorities, or because of family considerations. Still others leave because of organizational politics. Many leave because they want to earn big bucks. All of these are valid reasons to separate.

In conducting research for this book, we engaged a group of Interview Subjects who had successfully transitioned from their careers at CIA, NGA, NSA, FBI, State Department, U.S. Treasury, the ODNI and the Military about their own career transitions. Here's what they had to say about their own reasons for making "the Big Decision" to leave government service:

POLL QUESTION

Was there an event or specific circumstances that drove your decision to transition out? If so, what was it? How did you know that it was time?

Our Interview Subjects cited a number of specific reasons for leaving government. These included: Fit, Personal/Family Considerations, Career Advancement Stall, Workplace Politics/Ethics, Mandatory Retirement, Position Realignment, Contentment with Achievements, Desire/Need to increase income, or a combination of factors. Here are their comments:

Fit

> I could tell it was "time" as I no longer "fit" within the organization and was finding the decisions of institutional leadership difficult to comprehend.

Personal/Family Considerations

> I decided to enjoy life with my husband while I was able to, before the commute wore me out entirely. I hated leaving the friends at work, but certainly was ready to leave the work issues behind.

> At age 71, I wanted to experience more "me time".

> I knew I needed more time with family after a series of assignments that had been very demanding. My parents were in their late 80s, and I knew that I probably didn't have much time left with them. My mother died less than a year after I retired. I regret that I didn't leave sooner.

Career Advancement Stall

> I felt myself becoming toxic because my career advancement was dead-ended. I didn't like the kind of bitter person I was becoming.

> I knew it was time when I no longer agreed with the leadership and direction of my superiors. I saw a lack of

adequate respect for my service and accomplishments, and saw too many persons I felt were less deserving being promoted ahead of me. It was time for me to go.

> I knew I would not be promoted further; I did not think my immediate leadership valued my opinion or contributions any longer; I disagreed with several senior management decisions.

> I was in a job that was less satisfying than previous jobs, and I was at the point that I was eligible to retire with full benefits. Plus, I also felt that my past experiences and accomplishments were not being fully utilized.

Learn and Grow

> I needed a new challenge in a more innovative environment that would allow me to learn and grow.

> As a Senior Intelligence Service (SIS) officer, I went from one senior position to the other fixing similar problems. I wanted a change and to explore new opportunities.

> It was more a culmination of things such as feeling tired of the bureaucracy, feeling like I was performing the same old work over again, and feeling like I wanted a change.

Workplace Politics/Ethics

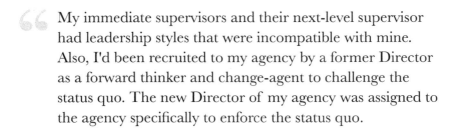 My immediate supervisors and their next-level supervisor had leadership styles that were incompatible with mine. Also, I'd been recruited to my agency by a former Director as a forward thinker and change-agent to challenge the status quo. The new Director of my agency was assigned to the agency specifically to enforce the status quo.

I saw unevenly applied and enacted policy changes in the organization, changing dynamics regarding organizational and leadership loyalties to the individual, and perceived shifting culture. This led me to strongly consider retirement and to "pull the trigger".

Although I held senior positions at the Agency, I didn't see a 'next step' assignment that interested me. I was put off by change in the political administration where there appeared to be a disrespect for the Intelligence Community to include leadership styles that berated senior officials—at various levels. I also had a sense of 'been there & done that'. It was time to go. After all, life is short.

I had issues with my immediate supervisors in terms of ethics and technical competence. I felt that they failed to respect (grasp) the Community nature of my position. Also, I had been muzzled from speaking publicly because I fiercely advocated for horizontal integration across the community, and the new Director was more comfortable with stovepipes.

Mandatory Retirement

Because I was not promoted to higher Military rank, by law, I had to retire from active Military service.

I faced mandatory retirement. I was extremely gratified by the career and experiences I had, and it was time for others to have the privilege I did.

Position or Skills Realignment

I decided to leave upon the elimination of my section as a separate entity, when I was transferred to another role.

I had 30 years in government, and I led a reorganization that changed my position.

I would have stayed if my work unit would have extended me for a fifth year; otherwise I was done and excited about a new career in teaching.

The Agency had started to move in very technical directions that would have required an investment in up-skilling.

Content with Achievements and No Drive to Stay

No other job was as interesting as the one I held.

I had reached the 30-year milestone in my career and concluded that there was nothing more I had aspired to accomplish and wanted to be challenged in the private sector.

My final assignment was such a highlight in my career; I had experienced incredible professional flexibility, reach, and influence; creative problem solving across directorates and staff; and impact at a larger scale than in any previous position. I knew it was time to go when I found myself struggling with the idea of being in another big leadership position, with the prospect of more long hours, a lot of bureaucracy and politics, and feeling out of step with current leadership team.

Desire/Need to Increase Income

When considering my long-term financial goals, moving to contractor status was the best option for me.

(I was attracted by) the ability to draw a pension in addition to working a job that could pay equal to or significantly more than my previous government position.

Our Interview Subjects were mainly propelled to leave Government Service after having stalled in their career advancement, having achieved a sense of accomplishment at a certain point, having some personal/family considerations that were taking priority, and/or having some ethical or political differences with workplace leaders.

Do you have some of these same issues/questions facing you in your career? Now it is your turn to evaluate your own reasons to exit.

WORKSHEET 1

IS IT TIME?
ASKING YOURSELF
SOME HARD QUESTIONS

In considering whether this is the "right time" for *you*, ask yourself some hard questions about why you are thinking of separation. This exercise can help you evaluate practically and take some of the emotion out of your decision-making. Think honestly about the specific reasons why you are now considering separation, and possibly searching for a new career. This self-reflection will help you better understand what *has not* worked well in your past career and mostly importantly the *why*. Now you can focus your sights on what you *do* want from your next steps. Reflection will also prevent you from choosing future work that does not play to your strengths and will help you avoid repeating mistakes of the past (by the way, *everyone* has made them). It will give you important language to use in interviews to explain why you are looking for a career change. Prospective employers value this sort of candor and self-reflection.

Some questions to consider:

What is driving your desire to make a career change? How long have you been thinking about it?

Was there a recent event/change that acted as a breaking-point, or has this been something you have been considering for a while, (i.e., are you driven by a genuine desire to seek change or this a reaction to a recent change/event only?)

Have you lost enthusiasm for your work? Can you pinpoint why?

In what ways did your career negatively impact your personal life?

What was not ideal about your career?

Are you changing to leave a bad situation? What was bad about it?

Did you reach mandatory retirement? How do you feel about being required to leave?

Did you have an unexpected life experience that changed your mindset? What was that?

Do you have family obligations (eldercare, for example) that are driving your decision?

Do you have a desire to do more with your life or your career? What is missing?

Did a personal or family illness alter your perspective?

What are your biggest fears about transitioning out of government?

4

HUMAN FACTORS IN CAREER TRANSITION

It is completely normal to have fears and potential second-thoughts about leaving government. Most transitioning employees worry about making wrong decisions and mistakes. Some wonder whether they are resilient enough for the change. Others worry whether their pension will be enough to sustain them (and their family) for up to 50 years. Some worry about unexpected outcomes from the decision to go, and are concerned about the impact of their separation on their mental and physical health. These are all valid concerns. However, overwhelmingly, the Interview Subjects explained that nearly all their fears were unfounded, and said that they were pleasantly surprised by their level of health and happiness on the "outside".

Here's what our Interview Subjects had to say about a wide range of human factors in career transition, from natural worries and concerns, to mental and physical health issues, to the most surprising and positive outcomes. In this chapter, we will discuss a wide range of Human Factors.

- In Human Factors Part 1, we address fears, second thoughts, mistakes, miscalculations, misperceptions, regrets, what you might miss the most, and unexpected outcomes from leaving government service.

- In Human Factors Part 2, we address mental and physical health, and resiliency.
- In Human Factors Part 3, we discuss the most positive outcomes and surprises, the biggest personal takeaways, and the best parts of life outside the Federal Government.

HUMAN FACTORS PART 1

In this section, we will discuss the scarier parts of making the decision to separate: fears, second thoughts, mistakes, miscalculations, misperceptions, regrets, what you might miss the most, and unexpected outcomes.

Personally speaking, the decision to leave government might have been the scariest decision that I ever made. I knew no other life. I went to work for the CIA at age 22 (directly out of college) and never held a professional position in the private sector prior to government service. Therefore, when considering retirement (or resignation), I was very afraid of what I didn't know. I wondered how my skills inside government would translate to a different organization. It was hard to visualize the kinds of problems that existed in a business that I could help solve. I did not know the business and finance jargon. Running operations, and tracking terrorists seemed very far removed from producing and selling a product or service. We had a common mission and camaraderie in government that I worried would not exist in a for-profit environment. I was anxious that I would not fit in…that with no graduate business degree or concrete business experience, I would look silly. Even though I would receive a pension, I was afraid of the loss of my current level of income and whether we would be able to maintain our lifestyle if I didn't land something else. I was also afraid that I would regret leaving and would want to go back. This is a stressful time in life. Relax! As it turned out, none of these worries were validated in my case.

Fear of the unknown and anxiety about how to translate your government skills can be an influencer for many people in determining their first step out of government. As you think about what is making you anxious, consider these questions:

- *What is scary for you about leaving the government sector completely? Of those elements that scare you, can you influence and control some of them? Which ones and how? What do you see as a worst-case scenario?*

- *What is exciting about the possibility of leaving? What do you see as a best-case scenario? What can you do to influence and control the outcome?*

Like all human beings, our Interview Subjects had their own fears and anxieties about leaving government. They talk below about their own fears and concerns about separation.

<u>FEARS</u>

POLL QUESTION

What were your biggest fears about separation? Were those fears realized? Did you have any regrets after making the decision to separate?

Several Interview Subjects mentioned fears about finances, worry about the ability to generate their own clients if self-employed, and concern about finding the right "fit" in a next position. Three other common themes also emerged when our Interview Subjects discussed their biggest fears about separation from the Federal Government. The majority of responses about transition fears focused on "loss", specifically losing personal and professional relationships, losing a sense of identity, and loss of a sense of purpose.

While fearing the loss of relationships and loss of identity are normal for anyone transitioning out of a long-term career situation, fearing the loss of purpose is especially strong in government servants, whose motivations and loyalty to their employer tend to be strong and highly ideological. Wanting to serve others and protect our national security are strong motivators and drivers. It is logical to fear the loss of such a strong life's purpose.

Loss of Important Relationships

> I worried about loss of relationships and close friendships when I transitioned out. What I discovered instead was that my good Agency friends will always be there. On top of that, my peripheral contacts inside the Agency and the broader Intel Community have been immensely helpful and friendly on the outside. They have mentored me, promoted my business, helped me solve problems, and found time to broaden and deepen our friendships. While we see each other less frequently, the continuation of our "tribe" has been a very positive and unexpected benefit of my separation. Perhaps we no longer suffer from the petty rivalries and competition that is part of inside life.

Loss of Identity

> I felt as though I was giving up more than a job—that I was giving up an important part of my identity. It took a few months to get past that feeling of loss.

> I was fearful of my ability to succeed outside the government. I was fearful of my ability to manage a

nonprofit organization, having had zero education, training, or experience to do so. I had made successful significant and nontraditional professional leaps before. This was comforting and imbued me with confidence, yet this leap outside the 'cocoon' of the military/government was the most daunting. I thrived in my new position for a decade, so my fears weren't realized.

Loss of Purpose

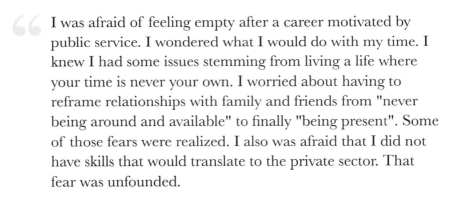 I was afraid of feeling empty after a career motivated by public service. I wondered what I would do with my time. I knew I had some issues stemming from living a life where your time is never your own. I worried about having to reframe relationships with family and friends from "never being around and available" to finally "being present". Some of those fears were realized. I also was afraid that I did not have skills that would translate to the private sector. That fear was unfounded.

I knew I would miss the sense of mission, and, after watching a superhero movie, I realized that helping keep America safe from the bad guys was a driving force for me. I knew I needed to find that again in retirement.

SECOND THOUGHTS

POLL QUESTION

If you ever had "second thoughts" or regrets after submitting your papers to separate, how did you handle that?

The vast majority of our respondents had no second thoughts at all about their decision to leave. The few who did have second thoughts provided the following comments on the topic:

> I had very serious regrets after full retirement, but did not understand at first why I was so sad. After speaking to a close friend who had retired at the same time and was experiencing the same sadness, we realized that we missed *being needed*. In our jobs, we spent all day, every day, solving problems for our large teams. We were no longer asked to do that, so we felt useless. Once we realized what was going on, we took steps to find ways to feel useful again.

> I had no significant second thoughts, but the process was extremely stressful for me. I had no idea how much my personal identity was tied to my previous employment. The change of jobs and uncertainty as to whether I would succeed was also a big stress. I knew it was the right decision, however.

> Yes and No. I miss the mission. I am certainly concerned about the group think inside the organization. Organization behavior is not to seek outside support which in my view they most desperately need.

Absolutely! You don't serve for decades without the 'job' becoming part of your identity, support structure, and social circle...no matter how hard you try to guard against that. Separating from it and the time immediately after is a significant life event. It is a divorce of sorts or a manner of loss, and thus emotions surrounding that are to be expected. There will be periods of depression, introspection, self-doubt, and anxiety—both about the future and what has been left behind. Whether these are mild to severe depends on the person's ability to recognize, process, and deal with this. Friend and family support structure, 'next chapter' mindset, and ability to stay active in pursuit of goals are all very necessary.

MISTAKES/MISCALCULATIONS/MISPERCEPTIONS

POLL QUESTION

What were your top transition "mistakes", miscalculations, or misperceptions?

Our Interview Subjects were asked about mistakes, miscalculations or misperceptions they made in connection with their decision to leave government. Some of their individual mistakes included: not negotiating a higher compensation package, not selecting the most financially advantageous date to retire, and not putting a contract in place to return to work prior to leaving. Another individual wished they had a clearer picture of what living on an annuity would really look like.

There were several key themes that came up in survey responses.

Those were: not taking enough time off; lack of resilience; not understanding how people with our backgrounds are perceived in the private sector; jumping too soon at a job opportunity out of fear; and underestimating the difficulty of setting up your own business, including the need for sales.

Taking a New Job out of Fear of not Finding one

> I went back to work too soon (about 90 days or less). I should have followed the advice to take more time off to really understand what I wanted to do. I think I was worried too much that I would lose the value of what I had to offer an employer.

Resilience and Introspection

> I didn't anticipate the stress involved in the transition. I barely slept for the first three months and probably went into depression.

> I did not adequately focus myself on what I wanted to do, rather than what I thought the market might want me to do and pay me for doing.

> My confidence in the strength of our organizational credentials and my executive status was a mistake. I had achieved a level of professional success and influence within an organization with a fairly solid reputation. I erroneously believed that my previous status would translate to recognition of my value by others in blind job posting

applications. You need a solid, network recommendation or someone on the 'inside' drawing attention to you specifically. Otherwise, odds are minuscule that submitting a blind resumé will result in more substantive conversations or interviews. The door is unlocked with the combination of a solid resumé, a helpful, networked introduction, and solid interview performance that generates rapport and interest from a prospective employer.

I did not anticipate the amount of competition for post-retirement positions, even in a strong economy. I also was not clear on pay—you have to have a realistic expectation on this, and it is incredibly difficult to figure out. I was afraid that people would react negatively to my intelligence background, when in fact, people were incredibly respectful and considerate.

Jumping at an Opportunity

There were several (mistakes): taking the first significant job offer because I was concerned no-one would hire me, following the money instead of my heart and instincts, believing all the myths about the private sector being more advanced than government (and especially leadership and innovation and flexibility), overcommitting my time to others in the non-profit and volunteer world, and wasting a lot of time on the job search instead of being more focused and reflective (which I did later to wonderful results).

I underestimated how much work it would be to become a small business owner and grow my executive coaching business, including navigating the legal requirements, setting up my website, advertising my services, following up on leads, and managing the financial aspects. I just wanted to coach frustrated professionals and help them! But business is work and takes time.

> I took me too long to realize that business is really just all about money and sales. While industry pretends to respect and get behind my Agency and their mission, it is really all about earning money from those agencies.

REGRETS

POLL QUESTION

If you accepted a position that you later regretted, what was the reason for your regret, how did you extricate yourself and how long did that process take, what lessons did you learn, and how did you recover from your experience?

For the most part, our respondents had very few regrets about what they chose to do after separation. Those who did have regrets noted one of the following reasons: They selected a position that was not the right fit for their interests or current circumstances; the organization evolved in a direction that was not consistent with the Interview Subject's values; they found that they had outgrown the position and wanted something more fulfilling; or they tried to replicate a past positive experience and found that things had changed. Here are the comments of the few who did have regrets:

Wrong Fit

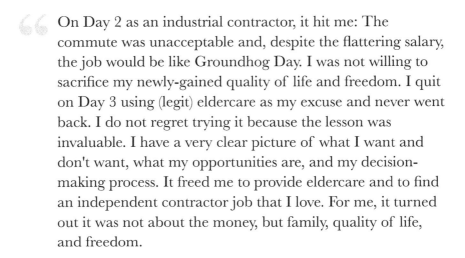

On Day 2 as an industrial contractor, it hit me: The commute was unacceptable and, despite the flattering salary, the job would be like Groundhog Day. I was not willing to sacrifice my newly-gained quality of life and freedom. I quit on Day 3 using (legit) eldercare as my excuse and never went back. I do not regret trying it because the lesson was invaluable. I have a very clear picture of what I want and don't want, what my opportunities are, and my decision-making process. It freed me to provide eldercare and to find an independent contractor job that I love. For me, it turned out it was not about the money, but family, quality of life, and freedom.

After two years in a job, I realized it was not exactly what I wanted. I did not regret the experience but knew this was not the job I could spend more time doing. I searched for a job that I was excited about and that fit more what I had a passion for.

Wrong Mission

I accepted an assignment in a former office. The assignment was a senior office level assignment in a different directorate. I loved the assignment; however, I also had regrets. The office had changed since I was there last. Rather than a Center in an Operational Directorate, it fell in a Directorate focused on Support—not a bad thing! However, the mission focus was different, and I found the directorate leadership styles to be difficult.

Several people told me prior to retiring that you would probably not stay at any one job for more than two or three years. I did not believe them and figured that if I found the perfect job, I would stay for five or ten years. My colleagues were correct, and the great thing about retirement is that you don't have to work at a place where you are unhappy. I worked for one company where I liked the management and my colleagues, but there were several employees in key positions that sought to undermine the company because they did not like the several new employees who were taking the company in a different direction. It became an issue of integrity, and I decided to extricate myself from this job. I spoke frankly to the CEO of the company and he understood.

DIFFICULT/UNEXPECTED OUTCOMES

POLL QUESTION

What has been the most difficult/most unexpected outcome of your separation from the Federal Government?

There were really no clear trends in the answers to this question. Our respondents had wide-ranging and candid comments to offer about the most difficult or most unexpected aspects of their separation from government. Given the variety of responses and lack of trends, nearly all responses are provided here for the benefit of readers:

Learning New Skills

The most difficult was learning new technical skills such as PowerPoint briefings.

I understood the politics and power structures inside of the Military and Federal Government, all the way to the highest levels across the executive and legislative branches. It's very different in industry/academia/nonprofit organizations, and I had to scramble to learn about all that very quickly in order to succeed.

Figuring Out What to Do With My Time

Learning what to do with "free time" once I left full-time employment at (a named U.S. Defense contractor) and started doing my own part-time consulting.

What you expect in a retirement job, after decades in a high pressure, high stakes, and dedicated environment where you regularly spend 12–16-hour days, is the ability to slow down a bit. What I have found is an eventual mission-creep on time. The more you dig in to your new career, the more time seems increase in both your devotion and contribution to it. At first, it seems a bit slow and relaxed.... That changes once you start becoming invested in it.

Getting Used to the Private Sector

My first job post-transition was a disaster, because I accepted it for all the wrong reasons (and I knew it, deep down), but it was invaluable learning lesson on listening to my instincts, recovery, and not burning bridges. Choosing between so many opportunities to learn and grow and wanting to spend time on everything and with everyone.

I would have to say not having enough time to enjoy with my husband. I tell everyone that if you can retire: Do it! Don't wait unless there is a financial reason for it. You never know what your future will bring so live each day to its fullest.

Difficulty helping government to be innovative, productive, and successful from the outside.

I am working harder now than in government service. Less job security. Success of business connected with the economy and other factors outside of your control.

I didn't realize how difficult it would be to find a meaningful job with reasonable compensation. I do find myself frequently questioning job preferences. Maybe at this point in life, it is good enough to punch the clock with little/no responsibility versus seeking a job (mission) that is meaningful. So I fly out to Denver for part-time work. The job compensates well. I still struggle whether it's the 'right' job for me at this point in life. Should I just punch it?

Getting used to a new organizational culture and working as a civilian without the rank and authority that my Military position had provided.

" It's taken longer than I thought it would take to get my business making money.

" Adjusting to the profit motivation of the private sector was the most challenging.

Adjustments to Personal Life

" Losing touch with friends who were still working.

" Moving and starting a new life.

" Discovering what truly excited me.

" Needing to rebuild/repair family relationships that had suffered because of my all-consuming career. While I was one of the lucky ones who stayed married to the same person throughout my government career, it was not without deep consequences to our relationship.

" I did not really expect that we would have to make so many adjustments to our own timeline to meet the needs of aging parents.

" If the phone doesn't ring for a couple weeks, it can be tough. I need to learn how to not over-schedule due to fear of not getting more work.

<u>MISSING THE OLD JOB</u>

POLL QUESTION

What do you miss most about your Federal Government career?

Think about what has mattered most to you in your government career. Often, the personal and professional relationships and the team/mission focus are what people believe they will miss most when they leave government service. People who serve a career in government service tend to be motivated by patriotism and working for a common cause. There is an overwhelming drive to serve our country. We often wonder: Will it be that way in my next place?

Two clear themes emerged in the survey when asking respondents what they missed most about their Federal Government career. Government servants most value their *relationships* in the workplace with high-caliber, highly motivated, patriotic colleagues. They also treasure the common *mission* that national security and policy jobs provide. It is natural that the People and the Mission would be the overwhelming responses in the survey. The Interview Subjects also provided some other key things that they missed as well.

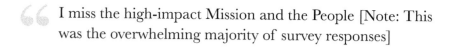 I miss the high-impact Mission and the People [Note: This was the overwhelming majority of survey responses]

Saying where I work ... the pride and the attachment to a venerable employer. I miss having that. It has been since March, 1976 that I was attached to the State Department thru my husband or thru my work. That is hard to let go. I have enormous feelings of attachment to State and the good work it does around the world.

> I sometimes miss the gravitas and authority that Military rank provided.

> Being proud of belonging to the civil service. Meeting new colleagues and watching the junior officers grow.

> Having insights on current issues that the public does not have.

> I do miss the direct involvement in activities which have a major impact on U.S. security and policies.

> I miss the adrenaline of operations, and the fulfillment of directly being able to impact the safety and security of the nation and our allies.

HUMAN FACTORS PART 2

Next, we will discuss other sensitive issues surrounding the decision to separate. These include mental and physical health, and resiliency in times of change.

MENTAL AND PHYSICAL HEALTH

Sometimes you hear stories about people who retire or leave a long-term job, go into a rapid decline, and then just drop dead. This is often attributed to the sudden change in their routine, which causes health issues, whether mental or physical. Some people find themselves feeling depressed and aimless and not needed. In this section, our Interview Subjects discuss the impact of their government separation on their mental and physical health, and provide tips on developing resiliency so that your upcoming change in routine is not such a shock.

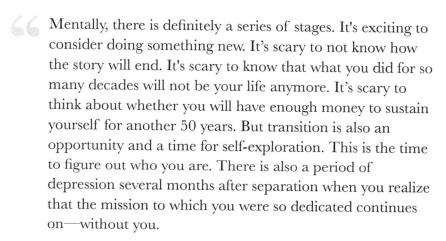

> Mentally, there is definitely a series of stages. It's exciting to consider doing something new. It's scary to not know how the story will end. It's scary to know that what you did for so many decades will not be your life anymore. It's scary to think about whether you will have enough money to sustain yourself for another 50 years. But transition is also an opportunity and a time for self-exploration. This is the time to figure out who you are. There is also a period of depression several months after separation when you realize that the mission to which you were so dedicated continues on—without you.

Some government agencies help their departing employees understand that they will go through mental health stages upon their departure from a long-term career. Others give it less attention. In speaking with friends who have moved beyond a government career, many spoke honestly about going through some emotional "rough patches". In order to understand how widespread these feelings are, this question was added to the survey.

Overwhelmingly, survey respondents were *very positive* about the impact of their transition on their physical and mental health. Less stress and more time to exercise and pursue personal interests and wellness led to a much greater sense of well-being in nearly all respondents. Many respondents felt "exhilarated" and "liberated" upon departure. The vast majority of survey respondents answered that their mental and physical health vastly improved. Some provided more nuanced responses, however, which are included below for the benefit of readers.

In terms of mental health, it was not always smooth sailing. While almost all Interview Subjects commented positively on their physical health post-separation, several respondents were very candid about going through mental health "stages" in their transition where they felt some emotional lows. This is an important fact that readers will want to be prepared for. Interview Subjects discussed the mental health challenges and some offered suggestions for managing those stages.

POLL QUESTION

What was the impact of your initial career transition on your mental health? On your physical health?

Mental Health: The Positives

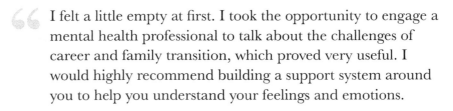

I felt a little empty at first. I took the opportunity to engage a mental health professional to talk about the challenges of career and family transition, which proved very useful. I would highly recommend building a support system around you to help you understand your feelings and emotions.

The day I turned in my badge and drove off the compound, I had a momentary panic attack because I knew I could not get back in. That was quickly followed by a profound sense of relief when I realized I did not have to go back in. That is when I knew, definitively, that I had made the right decision. It was freeing, and I could viscerally feel the imaginary weight falling off my shoulders. I slept so well that night— and better than I had in years. Other than the stress of finding a job, I took the time to clean my house out and reorganize (a bit compulsive, but it was my personal transition), I rediscovered the joy of being physically active again (kayaking, biking, a walk in the evening, and a regular workout routine that I was not trying to jam into work schedule). My husband and I became more socially active, reconnecting with friends and family, we started planning vacations and being more intentional about our down time. In essence, we discovered what having a life really meant. This was good for us, for me, mentally, emotionally, and physically and I have not let go of that in the six years since I retired.

It was excellent initially. I was happier than I had been in a long time and got in good shape physically. I cut back on drinking, got more engaged and active socially. I did discover that there is another transition point three years in, as many retirement books warn.

The career transition was a positive impact on my mental health. Can you say less stress? Also, a positive impact on my physical health as I frequented the local gym. I pursued home projects to keep me busy/active—although the 'honey do' list has dried up. Keeping busy is a challenge, but my spouse and I are trying to pursue things of mutual interest that will keep us active. We also need to invest in the local community. We are considering where best to apply our talent to help the community.

I'm blessed that I have a large network of women with whom I'm able to talk when I'm "down/blue". Being a single woman, I do worry about being alone. I pray more and find comfort being able to talk with my parish priest.

Mental Health: The Challenges

At first, there were pretty high levels of stress and anxiety, because you are in uncharted waters and leaving a relatively known, predictable, and stable environment. Secondly, unless you are moving directly from your last job into your new one, the financial question starts to loom large, because it takes entirely too long for your retirement pay to kick in. This can have negative impacts both mentally and physically. Once you are in that 'next step' and have spent a bit of time there and start to feel like you 'get it,' then things start to level off.

I mentioned feeling depressed at first, but I'm getting over that with time as I add structure to my days, work toward goals, and cross things off my list.

Transitioning was one of the most difficult periods of my life mentally and physically. I had trouble sleeping, and my blood pressure went through the roof. I probably suffered from depression given the uncertainty and my strong sense of identity connected to government work. I lost a lot of weight.

I'll admit that retiring, moving, and finding myself in a place where I didn't have any work friends, kid-school friends or other friends threw me off my game and I had a hard time reconciling myself to the possibility that "this was all there is." Physically, I gained weight because food is where I go when I'm sad.

The new challenges of working in a different agency and in a different capacity have been both mentally stimulating and, at times, draining. Lots of change at once—that is sometimes a bit overwhelming.

Physical Health

> Very positive! I felt exhilarated, liberated, and pursued things that I loved to do, but hadn't done for years. For example, I am rowing (my favorite sport by far) again almost daily, racing competitively.

> Big boost to positive mental and physical health. I got in much better physical shape which made me feel great. And, although I did not think I had a lot of stress, the stress of the job was obvious after it was gone!

> Physically, the transition was a great time to set priorities in terms of personal fitness and weight management. It was a time to try new things and enjoy friends around activities that you never had time for before.

> I feel much less stress. I am working out again with a personal trainer and take weekly yoga and Pilates classes.

Resilience

> Resilience means knowing how to cope in spite of setbacks, or barriers, or limited resources. Resilience is a measure of how much you want something and how much you are willing, and able, to overcome obstacles to get it. It has to do with your emotional strength.

Dr. Tony Alessandra, behavioral and communication expert.

POLL QUESTION

Are there things you could have done to make yourself more resilient prior to leaving service?

When faced with big decisions, such as a career transition, emotional strength is highly beneficial given the amount of change you are facing and the uncertainties about the future. Are there ways to prepare yourself to handle these inevitable stresses in a career transition? Here are some of the responses of the Interview Subjects on this question:

> I should have talked with more recent retirees about their own experiences. This would have made it less scary.

> I should have explored more of the options, to believe in my capabilities and abilities and how they would translate to the commercial market place.

> Good word... resilient.... Hmmm, I imagine that I would have started doing things to make myself more marketable and prepared much sooner. When I became eligible to retire, maybe I would have joined some professional organizations and achieved certifications that were useful. Secondly, I imagine I would have maybe taken a few courses to achieve some business acumen and lexicon so new terms and methods of analyzing a situation weren't completely foreign to me. While I did start to develop a private sector network, I would have been much more aggressive in that regard and diversified it. By diversify, I mean not just retirees in the private sector who come from same background as myself (Intel, Law Enforcement, etc.). Also, upon attaining retirement eligibility, I would have started to court Headhunter and placement firms. Finally, though difficult, I

really would have tried to build up a financial cushion that would allow for 3–4 months of relative security at your current cost level. I think going into the retirement/job hunting phase, if I had felt that I had the proper private sector certification credentials, a financial safety net, and a bit of knowledge regarding business lexicon and methodology, my comfort level would have been greater.

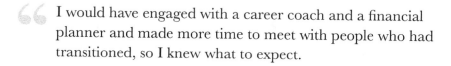 I would have engaged with a career coach and a financial planner and made more time to meet with people who had transitioned, so I knew what to expect.

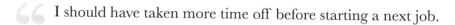 I should have taken more time off before starting a next job.

HUMAN FACTORS PART 3

<u>SUCCESSFUL TRANSITION OUTCOMES</u>

In Human Factors Part 3, we will discuss the best parts of the decision to separate: the positive surprises, biggest personal takeaways, and the best parts of life outside the government.

What do retirees and others departing from government say now about their life after separation? Again, it's overwhelmingly positive. The key to happiness seems to be looking at your transition as an *opportunity* to reinvent yourself, to spend more time with family and friends, to focus on fitness, to get involved in charitable causes, to have work-life balance, to travel at your own pace, and to learn new things. (In my case, I ventured out to the local community center, took a class in woodworking and learned how to use power tools to make and fix things—who knew!?) Doing some up-front assessment of your dreams, your bucket list, and your hidden interests will enable you to pursue new things that will be both fulfilling and rewarding.

POLL QUESTION

What were the biggest surprises for you, personally and professionally (both positive and negative), after leaving government?

There were several recurring themes in response to this question. Many respondents discussed their surprise at having much less stress. Others talked about loving their independence and valuing control over their time. Many commented on the excitement of finding so much to learn and to do—that there is actually a life after work.

As discussed in the Mental Health section, one respondent said her biggest surprise was the shock of not feeling useful or needed anymore. This is a common issue with separating Federal Government employees, but also with nearly anyone leaving a long-term job situation.

> I was surprised that, as eager as I was to retire from the Foreign Service, I found myself terribly unhappy a few weeks later. I finally figured out that I missed the feeling of being useful—and I missed working with such exceptionally talented and hardworking Foreign Service colleagues.

> I had not realized how very stressful our lives had been while employed at the Agency. After decades of pressure and 24/7 availability, it was wonderful to discover work-life balance, new hobbies, to learn new things, and to make new friends who did not care one bit (or ever ask about) what you had done before. I have enjoyed becoming a "normal person".

> There is a whole world out there of possibility and opportunity! The great surprise of so much to learn and do and people to meet.... Having the time and flexibility to pursue personal and professional interests and (to act) when opportunities arise.

Instead of losing work friends, I gained/regained more. Instead of losing mission, I gained/regained my real life. It opened-up a whole world of opportunities outside of intelligence. I learned what is enough to live on. Suddenly "things" don't mean as much. My values changed. It truly feels like a second chance at life. The only negative is learning how to manage private income and taxes after 33 years of very stable income.

Personally, I found the disruption to long-standing friendships and relationships surprising. Most of my friends were other senior military officers. Once we were all out, we went our separate ways. We no longer had the organization as a bond and each went in different directions. Maintaining those friendships has taken a lot more work than I thought.

That one can live comfortably on a government retirement. That family is so sustaining.

My network is far wider and deeper than I realized, and I am grateful for the number of people who have been willing to help me. I try to do the same for others when they retire.

I wasn't prepared for feeling a little depressed after "retirement." There were days early on when it was hard to get out of bed.

I think the single biggest 'ah-ha' moment for me was—even though I transitioned to a nonprofit which was focused on helping the government (and industry, and academia)— how quickly the door closed behind me. It was (and remains) incredibly difficult to keep tabs on people, leadership changes, emails, phone numbers, organizational changes, etc. The government is remarkably opaque even when it isn't trying to be.

MOST POSITIVE TRANSITION OUTCOMES

POLL QUESTION

What has been the most positive outcome from your transition?

Reflecting upon their lives post-government, Survey Respondents were asked to comment on the most positive outcome from their career transition. Several themes emerged in this area. Many respondents commented on how wonderful it is to have a life with much less stress, and with a higher level of physical fitness. Others were energized by having the freedom and flexibility to pursue things they loved, and to explore new knowledge. Learning was a significant theme. In several cases, respondents had started their own businesses and found it exciting to learn new skills and grow their knowledge in areas previously unexplored. Respondents also often commented on the positive aspects of having the time to deepen relationships with family and friends. Several also mentioned financial security as a significant positive from their transition. Here's what some of them had to say:

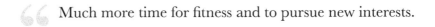 Much more time for fitness and to pursue new interests.

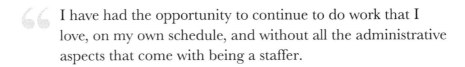 I have had the opportunity to continue to do work that I love, on my own schedule, and without all the administrative aspects that come with being a staffer.

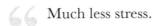 Much less stress.

" Building a life with my husband in a way that we never had the opportunity to do, as we were both consumed by demanding careers and were apart a lot; being planful and playful about our vacations and time together; meeting so many new and interesting people who do so many interesting things; having time for friends and family, and especially those in need, which has been so special to us; discovering new interests and investing more time on ongoing interests that we could never pursue to the extent that we wanted; time with family, and especially the kids and grandkids; and having flexibility and spontaneity in our lives that we never had before; and so much more.

" I learned other business skills that I never thought I would engage in.

" Learning new things such as business/financials and how to scale a growing business. Meeting clients' needs. Solving problems for clients and making a complex problem simple for the client. Meeting new people. Working from home if possible. Making more income.

" Being totally relaxed and having a feeling that the world is my oyster. I can create a new life, one that has meaning, giving back and learning new things. It is exciting!

" I was most intrigued to do something new. I was fortunate in that my current employer found me. I am working in a field I love, even while learning new things about language technology and gaining new colleagues and meeting new people.

" I'm doing what I love and getting paid for it.

> More time with my family. The chance to eventually write and express my views in public. I now have my own company and speak to academic and government groups. It's fun!

> Becoming a businesswoman, though challenging, has been energizing. And focusing on my business helped me get over those initial down feeling after retiring.

Interview Subjects were then asked to comment on their biggest takeaway about themselves in the process of transitioning careers.

POLL QUESTION

What is your biggest takeaway about yourself in the career transition process?

Many responded with takeaways about their individual lifestyle and the best ways to keep themselves positive, happy and healthy. The most significant responses came from those who had made time to reflect and consider who they are as individuals beyond the workplace. This is not an easy process for Federal Government servants who are often unaccustomed to thinking about their own life values and deep motivators. The respondents who were better adjusted were those who were able to look at themselves as a whole person, and to de-link their profession/job title from who they are as an individual. This enabled them to move forward to pursue new interests and to learn new things. Much of this self-exploration process has to do with evaluating one's personal and professional values and thinking about what motivates you to be your best self. Later in the book, you will find several worksheets to help in your evaluation of what really matters to you personally, so that you can pursue next steps that will be fulfilling to you.

" I learned that I'm not defined by who I was when I was with the Government. For the last 23 years, I thought of myself as "an FBI agent." That's not me, that's what I did.

" You need to figure out who you are. This is the time. Hint: "Who you are" is *not* "What you do". (You are a whole person, not just a job title.) You are much more than an intelligence professional. Your life has many more dimensions that are meaningful, fulfilling, and waiting to be explored.

" To quote Brené Brown: 'I am enough, I have value, and I can choose how I want to spend my time and with whom.' HUGE! I rediscovered who I am outside of the CIA, what is important to me and motivates me unencumbered by requirements of mission and organizational bureaucracy, my values, the ability to pursue my passions and interests, how to leverage my strengths in ways that are most satisfying to me and having the impact that I want to have, how important relationships are to me and how I let them lapse because of work, and to learn and to grow in ways again that brought me energy and fulfillment.

" I once thought that I would work far longer than I did because I loved my job so much, and it was such a big part of who I was. However, I did not have any sense of loss of identity after retirement, and instead found that I had been burying desires to do other things that I never had time for.

" Who you are is not what you do! I had a wonderful career and am proud of what I accomplished, but we can all have a second symphony (and third and fourth) if we want to.

THE BEST PART OF NEW LIFE OUTSIDE OF GOVERNMENT

POLL QUESTION

What has been the best part about your new life outside of government?

As noted in other survey questions, Interview Subjects found a great many positives in their new lives outside of government. In responding to this question, the very best part of a new life outside of government trended toward three key areas: the gift of time, finding life balance, and the invigoration of taking on new challenges.

> Much more ME time (which includes time with family and friends.)

> Freedom to choose how I structure my life.

> Time!

> Meeting new people, making more money, doing something I enjoy.

> The learning and growth experience has been refreshing and awakening. New challenges provide energy. I'm proud of my past but am thrilled about the potential in the future.

> The liberating effect of stepping off the treadmill and away from the petty, bureaucratic politics so prevalent in Washington, DC.

> Discovery and adventure!

" Life balance. It's fantastic!

" I've gotten out of my comfort zone and have met wonderful new people and am growing my network. There is a whole new world outside the Federal Government.

THE PRACTICALITIES OF LEAVING — HOW TO GET READY

Career change means conducting self-reflection that will help you move forward toward a next step that is a good fit with who you are. This is the right time to take stock of your life: assessing your readiness, financially, practically, and emotionally.

In the pages that follow, you will find a series of exercises that may help you to evaluate whether (or not) you are ready to go emotionally, whether you are financially ready, and whether (or not) a second career is the right path for you.

FINANCES

This is a great time to step back and have a philosophical discussion with yourself about your life and about your vision for the future for yourself and your family. As you move ahead toward making "The Big Decision" to leave the Federal Government, it is a critical time to take stock of your financial picture and think about your resource requirements going forward. Don't let your departure be an impulse decision. Plan well in advance, so you have options and are not locked-in to stay somewhere longer than you wish because of debt, for example.

The 2020 Covid-19 global pandemic and resulting economic downturn highlighted the real importance of prioritizing expenses, living within your means, and eliminating debt as soon as practical. Those considering separation from government and those who were retirement-eligible who had cash savings, a pension, paid-off mortgages, and no recurring credit card debt, student debt, or car payments were far better off than others in this crisis. Try to make a low to no-debt lifestyle your ultimate goal before you separate.

FINANCIAL READINESS

POLL QUESTION

Did you feel prepared in terms of assessing your financial situation and having confidence that you could "make it" financially after retiring? How far in advance did you begin to plan financially for your departure from the Federal Government? Did you use a financial advisor or any specific financial tools to assess your financial readiness?

Responses to this question were varied. Recurring themes included: taking any agency-specific retirement/separation-planning training as soon as allowed (many people wished they had taken such courses sooner in their careers so that they could implement recommendations while still working.). Others discussed the importance of understanding your family budget and expenses (with a key message that *reducing or completely eliminating debt is very important in the years leading up to separation*). A family monthly budget calculation worksheet is included here in this book. The third trend in response to this question was the importance of understanding

what you have in the Thrift Savings Plan (TSP) (Thrift) and other invest-
ments, and the use of financial advisors or online financial planning tools.
The group was split 50/50 on the use of a financial advisor versus using
online tools or doing their own evaluation of their financial situation.
Several people made quick decisions to separate, and did not feel that they
were financially well-prepared for the move. Most survey respondents
began financially planning 3–10 years prior to their separation.

> Yes, I felt prepared. The career transition classes offered by
> CIA allowed me to start preparing financially about 10 years
> before I retired. I did consult with a financial advisor before
> I submitted my retirement papers, so I felt confident that I
> was in good financial shape.

> A year or so before I became eligible, I used Quicken to look
> at several years' worth of living expenses and compare those
> figures with my estimated pension. I also had two pots of
> money, one in thrift and the other invested thru a financial
> advisor. I calculated how much each could provide me each
> year, should I need it.

> No, I was terrified about my financial situation. I had done
> no advance planning. It was a shock when the Secretary of
> State told us he would be leaving at the end of the
> administration. I decided virtually immediately that I would
> not stay under his successor.

> I was fairly well prepared, but I wish I had known and
> understood more about retirement programs, such as SEPs
> and 401(k)s. My CIA retirement annuity is one of the best
> and would take care of my wife and me for the rest of our
> lives, but I had a very shallow knowledge of retirement
> investment.

" Looking back, and knowing what I know now, I would have consulted a financial advisor earlier and built my own strategic plan about what I wanted my next phase of life to look like. However, I did not know that then, and I am not sure I could have articulated what I wanted my life to look like or my goals at the time of transition; the CIA had been my whole life and there was a whole world out there that I had no real experience with. I only knew I was ready for a change and had faith and confidence in my ability to make it work.

" Yes, I consulted a financial advisor and made certain that I could survive on just my annuity.

" With a paid off house, Foreign Service retirement annuity and investment in TSP we felt comfortable. We began to prepare 3 years in advance of separation.

" One of the most important keys to knowing if you are financially ready for retirement is having a solid grasp of your monthly expenses -- so keeping track of a month budget is something that is important to do throughout your life but particularly as you're nearing retirement. The budget can be as simple as an Excel spreadsheet that includes all expenses (in a monthly format) including expected travel. Most people don't want to go through the effort of fully understanding their monthly expenses and that makes it very challenging to have the confidence to know whether they are financially ready to retire or not.

AGENCY CAREER TRANSITION SUPPORT SERVICES

POLL QUESTION

If your agency provided Career Transition services to prepare you for separation, which of those services was most valuable to you? If your agency did not provide Career Transition services, what support do you wish you had been given?

Survey respondents spoke very favorably of the career transition training and services provided by CIA and to some extent by the Military, State, and NSA. Other agencies did not provide the same level of support to their departing employees. Employees separating short of retirement did not receive help to facilitate a smooth transition. Several respondents commented that it would have been more beneficial to have elements of the transition training, particularly the financial planning information, at mid-career. Some commented that their training lacked information on how to develop a Value Proposition (more on that later).

My Agency's Career Transition Program was excellent. It has since been scaled back, but they played an important function in educating people about "life after" and the important things to think about. They had terrific speakers about topics I had never thought about.

Because I was resigning (not retiring) as a young senior executive, I was offered nothing in terms of transition services. I did seek out the assistance of the Ethics Counsel to issue an ethics letter to cover my transition discussions with industry (job search).

Yes, I participated in the Retirement Seminar that State offers, as well as the career transition workshops—a three-month commitment. Both segments provided useful advice —that I wish I had been given 20 years earlier in terms of financial planning. I appreciated the instruction on resumé writing.

" Career Transition was excellent when I retired. The speakers were good and helpful. I would only suggest that some of the speakers we had should be given at mid-career, so you can be better prepared for retirement. I realize no one actually thinks about retiring until the time comes, but if a course was given at mid-career, it might help people. Especially since people are now in Federal Employee Retirement System (FERS)—I was fortunate to be on Civil Service so did not have to use my Thrift savings as part of my annuity.

" The Military provided mandatory transition training. It was more thought-provoking than helpful in terms of skill development. It provided a means to consider various options but was pretty poor in terms of resumé preparation, interview skills, and the process of finding a job. The Military built the course to fit all ranks rather than having specialized training for senior people retiring from a full career versus younger service members who were simply moving to civilian life after a few years of service.

" NSA provided retirement seminars that were useful. There were no career transition services as such, and the seminars given in the weeks before you actually retired, although interesting, were a little too late.

" I enjoyed working with a Transition Counselor. There were several points I needed to hear 1) You climbed the corporate ladder so there isn't a need to continue after you retire; 2). It's time to concentrate on me—health, hobbies, enjoyment and 3) I need a plan post-retirement. What was I going to do? What was important to me? What were my hobbies? I suspect people who read this are thinking "Well duh! In my career, I was dedicated and committed to mission. Mission drove my work ethic, as many in the same situation can relate to, and I became a workaholic during my career. Usually the long hours were at the detriment of time for health, family, and friends.

SMOOTHING THE TRANSITION

POLL QUESTION

What is the most helpful thing you did to make the separation go smoothly?

Looking back, Interview Subjects evaluated what actions they had taken to make their separation go most smoothly. Three key recommendations emerged from their experiences. The most prevalent response was the value of speaking with others who had already transitioned to get their advice and tap into their network. Another popular response was to practice interviewing. Finally, several respondents noted that counseling/coaching had been beneficial to help them assess themselves and their range of next steps.

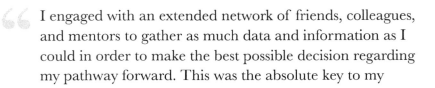 I engaged with an extended network of friends, colleagues, and mentors to gather as much data and information as I could in order to make the best possible decision regarding my pathway forward. This was the absolute key to my

smooth transitions - the ability to gather a broad array of data and information, assess it clearly, and execute against the results of that assessment. It was very much applied operational intelligence.

> I read a book and did the exercises in a book entitled *Acing the Interview* by Tony Beshara. It's a little dated, but an excellent book about the process of interviewing, who is involved and what their motives are, the phases of an interview, and some of the more difficult questions a candidate might face. As I had not been through a job interview in 30 years, this was extremely insightful, much better than the "class" the Military offered.

> About 18 months before I retired, I started talking to colleagues who had retired before me and contacts in industry about options and opportunities. It helped me narrow my focus to corporate board service, and I interviewed with two different bank boards within six months of retirement.

> I had never really interviewed for a job, and before I retired (and after retiring), I interviewed for a number of jobs just to get the practice of interviewing, learning how to describe my value to that company, knowing my monetary value, and learning to express diplomatically where, when, and what jobs I was prepared to accept.

> I used a coach to think through my priorities and goals.

TRANSITION TIPS

It is commonly recognized that most people stay in their first job after leaving the Federal Government for less than 18 months. In the case of the Interview Subjects, they tended to stay in their first job somewhat longer. In any case, don't become paralyzed by the decision-making process for your next move because you are afraid to make a mistake and get stuck somewhere for the long-term. If you choose a path that does not end up being the best fit for you, take that experience and the lessons learned and find something else you want to do more. That's a fairly typical experience.

Anxiety about loss of mission and loss of friendships is a big thing in our community. It is beneficial to develop an advance plan to manage the anxiety of anticipated loss of friends and mission. It also pays big dividends to step-up your networking efforts and get practical about the steps to a smooth departure. These practical steps might include:

√ **Ensure that you have outside contact information** to reach those colleagues and friends who mean the most to you. Make the effort before you leave service to build your contact list and ensure that your friends also know where to find you and how. You can begin by setting up a professional-sounding email address and creating some low-cost business cards for yourself. The cards should contain your name, an email address you will check regularly and a contact phone number. For the email address, use some variation of your name such as *Bill.Jobseeker@gmail.com*, (*not Harleyboy@aol.com, ilovepoledancing@yahoo.com*, or *puppylover@msn.com*.

√ **Become active/more active on professional and social media sites** such as Facebook and LinkedIn to get and stay connected. The abundance of information available on the internet can help you find and reconnect with old friends. This can be uncomfortable for some of you who are accustomed to living in the shadows. However, your "less shadowy" colleagues have been using social media for decades, and your failure to do so will disadvantage you professionally, and can negatively highlight you more than making appropriate use of the tools. Be thoughtful about what you want your professional and social media profiles to look like online before you post anything. More on this topic later in the Networking and LinkedIn section of the book.

√ **Keep the network alive.** Join your organization's "alumni association", as well as joining other organizations where current and former Intelligence Community (IC) members are involved. Consider joining the Intelligence and National Security Alliance (INSA), Washington Executive, the CIA Retirees Association (CIRA), or attending events or volunteering at the International Spy Museum.

√ **Be clear about what you can say and not say about your previous career**, in person, on a resumé, and on social media. Get that guidance in writing if you can.

√ **Talk with other retirees about their final employment status when they retired.** In general, IC agencies are now advising nearly all employees to be (or become) overt employees when they retire. It simplifies the benefits process through OPM (and simplifies your life, frankly). Just because you retire overtly does not mean that you need to go around and set the record straight with all your family and friends. It can be awkward, especially if you have foreign national family members. However, experience has shown that family, friends and business contacts, if they really need to know exactly who your former employer was, are highly respectful and generally ask very few questions.

. . .

√ **Begin the paperwork process early** if your transition will require the approval of multiple components. In most government agencies, separation can be highly bureaucratic and the process can take many months.

√ **Consider the timing of your departure.** Consult with a retirement specialist within your organization. They can provide excellent advice on the best dates to retire to maximize your financial situation. Generally, people in the IC retire at the end of the calendar year in order to maximize their payout of unused annual leave and service credit for unused sick leave. This can affect your pension, so don't make your retirement date decision in a vacuum.

√ **Bank some money to live on prior to your retirement date**, because your first retirement check could take 6–8 weeks to arrive.

√ If you are divorced, **be clear about the potential impact** of the rights of any former spouse on your retirement benefits. In many situations, an ex-spouse is entitled to claim 50% of your pension, prorated for the period of time that you were married to them while in the Federal Government service. Also, understand your financial obligations to any minor children. Your retirement office can help with these questions.

√ If you intend to continue working in an industry that supports the Federal Government, **make sure that your security clearance is up-to-date**, including a polygraph if your job requires one. The more recent your clearance, the better your chances of being able to leverage it. If you are nearing time for a reinvestigation, you may wish to consider staying in until your new Background Investigation is complete and your clearance has been adjudicated. A fresh clearance gives you more options and can be used as a bargaining chip in your next career.

. . .

√ **Get an Ethics Letter** from your office legal counsel which specifies any restrictions on the kind of post-government work you can pursue. You may have a "cooling off" period of months-to-years if you are separating short of retirement, or if you are an SIS/SES officer. You may be banned from ever working on specific contracts over which you had decision-making authority as a Federal Government staffer. Check this out and be clear on any restrictions. Most government contracting companies require a copy of your Ethics Letter and clear guidance in writing from the Federal Government on any restrictions you may have before they can engage in even preliminary discussions with you about prospective employment. There are severe consequences for government-contracting companies if they do not follow these procedures, which could potentially include loss of existing contracts.

√ **Obtain guidance from your agency about your resumé,** including pre-clearing it with a Publications Review Board if applicable. Many separating intelligence employees draft an extensive resumé or Curriculum Vitae (CV) with a variety of skills emphasized and get this broad version cleared. This approach gives a separating employee plenty of cleared material to draw-upon later when drafting a tailored resumé for a specific position.

√ If you led a covert life or worked in an environment without cell phones, **be aware that there is a learning curve** regarding the pervasiveness of social media and use of technology.

√ **Get into the right frame of mind.** This is a critical element of a successful transition. Look at your transition as *an opportunity* to learn, to grow, to contribute to something new, and to re-energize your life. Transitions tend to be most successful if you retire/separate *to* something new, rather than retiring/separating *from* something. Create a set of new life goals.

WORKSHEET 2

FINANCIAL READINESS

A key element to separating from a secure position in any sector is financial readiness. Now is the time to evaluate your financial situation. Consider the following important questions:

What are your current and future financial requirements?

List your short term (next 5 years) financial needs here:

List your longer-term financial needs here:

Have you made a budget to determine your needs going forward?

Do you have a specific timeline to completely eliminate any debt?

Have you fully funded your childrens' college education if that is your intent?

Have you met with a financial planner to discuss the future?

Do you have an up-to-date will, and medical power of attorney? Is it current?

Have you thought about setting up a Trust? Do you understand the pros and cons?

Do you have an advance medical directive?

Have you weighed the pros and cons of Long-Term Care insurance? Do you understand when would be the most advantageous age to purchase this insurance if you decide it is right for you?

Have you discussed your end-of-life decisions with your loved ones?

———

These are all very serious topics. Make a checklist and don't be overwhelmed. Some of these items are quickly taken care of. Others will take a little time. If you go ahead and set up the appointments to meet with the right experts, you will have a big sense of accomplishment already. Your Agency may have a list of experts you can call upon as a resource, including some former government colleagues who are now lawyers, financial planners, investment specialists, etc.

WORKSHEET 3

TO WORK OR NOT TO WORK?

Are you considering the idea of a second career following separation?
Answer the following questions to help you evaluate potential next steps.

How long do you plan to work in a second career?

How did you set that timeline?

Do you want to work full-time, part-time, on-call (project based)?

Do you need to be employed and receive employer-sponsored benefits, or do you/can you consider independent contractor (1099) opportunities?

If your long-term financial needs were being met, would you still want to work? Why or why not?

Does paid work fill some intrinsic needs that would not be met by being retired? What are those needs?

- *Social interaction for mental health?*
- *Having a feeling of influence?*
- *Feeling needed?*
- *Feeling important/significant?*
- *Feeling that nobody else could do the job as well as you can?*
- *Needing to contribute to a mission that is bigger than yourself?*
- *Other*

Write down the reasons that you believe you need to continue working (beyond financial).

How else could these needs be met besides taking another full-time job?

How and when will your personal long-term goals be met if you continue working?

WORKSHEET 4

UNDERSTANDING YOUR MONTHLY
FAMILY BUDGET

When was the last time that you actually mapped out your current expenses and income? This exercise can help you understand your financial picture going forward.

Monthly Budget

Gross Income

Salary & Wages	$_____ __%
Child Support & Alimony	$_____ __%
Pension & Social Security	$_____ __%
Rental Income	$_____ __%
Investment Income: Dividends, Capital Gain	$_____ __%
Interest Income	$_____ __%
Other	$_____ __%
Total Gross Income	**$_____ __%**

Liabilities

Mortgage: Principal Home	$_____ __%
Property Taxes: Principal Home	$_____ __%
Rent & Fees: Principal Home	$_____ __%
Mortgage, Rent, Taxes, Fees: second Home	$_____ __%
Automobile Loan(s) or Lease(s)	$_____ __%
Home/Renters Insurance	$_____ __%
Child Support & Alimony	$_____ __%
Total Liabilities	**$_____ __%**

Taxes

Federal Income Taxes	$_____ __%
State & Local Taxes	$_____ __%
Personal Property Taxes Other Than Real Estate	$_____ __%
Other	$_____ __%
Total Taxes	**$_____ __%**

FICA and Medicare

FICA & Medicare: Individual	$_____ __%
FICA & Medicare: Spouse/ Partner	$_____ __%
Total FICA and Medicare	**$_____ __%**

Insurance

Life Insurance Premiums	$_____ __%
Health Insurance Premiums	$_____ __%
Long Term Care Insurance	$_____ __%
Auto Insurance	$_____ __%
Home Owners/Renters Insurance	$_____ __%
Other	$_____ __%
Total Insurance	**$_____ __%**

Transportation

Gas and Oil	$_____ __%
Maintenance and Repair	$_____ __%
License	$_____ __%
Public Transportation	$_____ __%
Parking	$_____ __%
Tolls	$_____ __%
Other	$_____ __%
Total Transportation	**$_____ __%**

Monthly Budget Continued

Household Expenses

Groceries	$_____ __%	Dentist	$_____ __%
Eating Out	$_____ __%	Prescription Drugs	$_____ __%
Clothing & Footwear	$_____ __%	Professional Fees, CPA, Legal	$_____ __%
Electricity, Gas, Fuel	$_____ __%	Education Expenses	$_____ __%
Water/Sewer	$_____ __%	Lawn Care Maintenance	$_____ __%
Trash Collection	$_____ __%	Recreation & Hobbies	$_____ __%
Household Services: Cleaning	$_____ __%	Entertainment, Movies, Concerts	$_____ __%
Home Maintenance & Repair	$_____ __%	HOA Fees	$_____ __%
Telephone	$_____ __%	Veterinarian & Pet Care	$_____ __%
Subscriptions/Memberships	$_____ __%	Vacation & Travel	$_____ __%
Gym Membership & Classes	$_____ __%	AAA Membership	$_____ __%
Cable, Internet	$_____ __%	Charitable Contributions	$_____ __%
Personal Care	$_____ __%	Other	$_____ __%
Child Care	$_____ __%	***Total Household Expenses***	$_____ __%
Doctor	$_____ __%		

Totals

Total Monthly Income	$_____
Total Monthly Expenses	$_____
Net Income/Cash Flow	$_____
Percentage Net Cash vs Income	__%

WORKSHEET 5

PROJECTING YOUR FUTURE
SALARY REQUIREMENTS

If you intend to work following separation, do you understand what your minimum salary requirements are for your next job? Use the information gained from Worksheet 4 to project your new salary needs in Worksheet 5.

Income

Pre-retirement income after taxes (monthly salary) $_____

Projected monthly pension after taxes   (minus) $_____

Social Security Income (as applicable)   (minus) $_____

***Income gap between pre-retirement and
post-retirement income*** $$_____

Expenses

Projected monthly family budget expenses (from previous
worksheet) $_____

Additional monthly financial goal expenses in retirement +
(fully find 401ks, fully fund 529 plans, additional monthly
payments to pay-off debt, such as mortgage) $_____

Total projected monthly expenses $$_____

Wants

Additional discretionary income required to support work/
life balance, such as travel fund; gym memberships; charitable
donations, and meals & entertainment

Total projected monthly expenses   (minus) $$_____

***Income gap + projected additional monthly expenses =
NEW SALARY NEEDS*** $$_____

PART III

AND NOW WHAT?
POTENTIAL PATHS TO CONSIDER

MAKING A PLAN

Although there are plenty of second career options available out there, you hear the most about (the very small number of) your former colleagues who are making big bucks as Senior Advisors to corporate leadership, C-Suite Executives, Risk Analysts and Business Developers for major defense contractors, banks, investment firms, and oil companies. When these organizations believe that someone will bring value to their bottom line, there is no limit to the wining-and-dining and courting they'll do to bring an attractive Intelligence Community, Senior Military, or Foreign Policy applicant with specific skills and network to the table. Deep expertise in physical security, cyber security, risk assessment, predictive analysis, and counter-terrorism brings value to some multinational power-house companies. However, these second career options are only for a select few with the right credentials and pedigree. They are very often very high pressure jobs with high-dollar new business targets that you must meet to be considered successful. Your colleagues who end up in these sorts of jobs often don't stay very long. Please manage your expectations and your inherent competitive drive. Your transition is your own and you are competing with no one. There are many "next step" options to consider that can be both rewarding and fulfilling!

Some questions to ask yourself when evaluating your options:

Are you interested in changing fields completely? Why or why not?

Are you considering a move to part-time employment? Why or why not?

Do you want to "retire retire" (i.e: retire completely)? What is attractive about this?

Do you want to work in the private sector or as an independent contractor supporting your old employer? What are your reasons for wanting to do so?

What would those scenarios look like for you?

Once you have made "The Big Decision" to leave, it's time to consider what you'd like to do next. Your options are many, and could include full retirement, pursuing another job or volunteering in some capacity. If you wish to continue working, either for financial reasons or to keep yourself engaged, you will want to evaluate whether that will work be full-time or part-time, paid or voluntary (or some combination thereof). If you opt for another job, will it be supporting your current government area of expertise, or are you interested in changing fields completely?

HAVING A SPECIFIC PLAN

POLL QUESTION

By the date of your separation, did you have a specific plan for what you would do next, or did you want to "test the waters" and explore options before making a firm decision?

How did your former colleagues decide what they wanted to do next? Did they have a specific plan? About half the respondents knew what they wanted to do at their separation date, and another half wanted to explore a variety of options before settling on a path. They wanted to "test the waters".

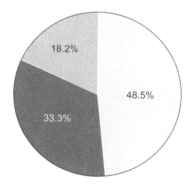

○ Had a specific plan for my next step at separation.

◉ Wanted to "test the waters" before settling on a next step.

◉ Other (each 3%)
  - I knew that I wanted to be employed for another 5-10 years but wanted to "test the waters" re the type of company (large or small) to be employed with.
  - No. I investigated options at the local University. However, I declined to pursue them because of the inadequate compensation.
  - I knew I wanted to pursue the "portfolio" approach of a variety of part-time positions. Corporate board service was at the top of my list. I had my resume cleared, was sharing it with contacts and was being very forthright about my interest in board service.
  - I had been assured by senior managment in DS, I would be brought on as a WAE once I applied, which I was.
  - Taking at least a year off before committing to anything more than volunteer or pro bono.
  - I had already begun interviewing and had several offers in hand. On the day I walked out, I already knew what I would be doing.

> By the date of your separation, did you have a specific plan for what you would do next, or did you want to "test the waters" and explore options before making a firm decision?

TAKING TIME OFF

POLL QUESTION

If you opted to take time off prior to beginning your job search, how much time did you take? Did that hinder your job search in any way? How did you use that time?

Many leaving government service elect to take some time off before starting a previously identified job, or even before initiating a formal job search campaign. More than half of our Interview Subjects took at least some time off prior to starting another job. It is generally a good idea to take a break if you can afford to do so financially. This "break" can provide valuable time to decompress, to travel, to reconnect with family and friends, and to provide needed help to your parents if they are still living. For those Interview Subjects who decided to work again, experiences were varied, but most took time off prior to beginning their new job and were very glad that they did. This enabled them to decompress and make a smooth transition with a clear mind. A few respondents took time off, but became restless at home and went back to work earlier than originally planned. For those Interview Subjects who did not take any time off between jobs, they unanimously now wish that they had done so.

 I took seven weeks off before starting my new job. This was negotiated with my new employer in advance, with the contract signed at the time that I retired. I used this time to travel abroad with my husband, and to take my mother on several trips to visit relatives. This time meant a great deal to my family. It was also incredibly valuable time for me to unwind and shift mental gears for the next phase of my life.

" I took not even one day off, which was a mistake. But I was terrified about the drop in my income and needed to make it up.

" I took off six months, three more than expected, but I was not ready to go back to work. Now that I look back, that should have been my first sign that I was not pursuing the right next step for me. I don't think it hindered my job search and certainly was the right thing for me: I used that time to decompress from a 32-year career, rethink my life goals and lifestyle, reconnect with family and friends, recommit to a healthier lifestyle, and try to figure out what I wanted to do when I grew up.

" I took two weeks between retirement and a new job start. I could have taken longer. My new employer was more than willing to let me. I was going crazy at home and needed to start the new adventure in order to begin relaxing about the pending change.

" I planned to take three months, and ended up taking six. Most fun I've ever had.

" I wish I had done so in retrospect. I would have arrived at my new position refreshed and renewed, and would almost certainly have done a better job of onboarding and taking the reins of the new organization if I was better rested/renewed/reinvigorated.

LENGTH OF A JOB SEARCH

POLL QUESTION

How long did it take you to find your first position outside of government?

For those readers who opt to pursue post-retirement employment, experience has shown that you may not walk out the door with a specific job waiting for you. Once you begin your job search in earnest, however, it shouldn't take long. For those who sought onward employment after separation, data shows that 82.6% of our respondents landed a position within six months. You will want to have a financial gap plan and resources in place to help you get through the estimated period until you begin your new opportunity. Here's the data from our Interview Subjects on their own experiences with the duration of their job searches:

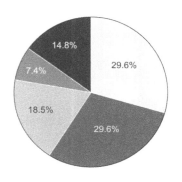

○ I moved immediately into a position I had already secured.

● It took 0-2 months to sign a contract and start a new job.

◔ It took 3-6 months.

◕ It took 6-12 months.

● Other (each 3.7%)

- I initially was interviewing for a part-time job at a think tank. I was to give a presentation several months after retirement. In the interim, though, I realized I no longer wanted to work, so declined to pursue the opportunity further.
- I found the position and then decided to retire.
- I started part-time contract work immediately.
- Taking a year off. Secured advisory positions on boards upon retiring.

How long did it take you to find your first position outside of government?

FINDING THE PERFECT FIT IN A NEXT JOB

POLL QUESTION

How long did you stay in that first position after separation?

Many people leaving the Federal Government do not stay in their next position forever! Don't worry about "making a mistake" in your first move. These are opportunities to learn about a new business and grow yourself and broaden your skills. This is part of the process to find the eventual "best fit". Many people who move to the corporate sector stay in their first job only a year or two, then move on to something else that interests them more. (Those who opt to go out on their own tend to stick with it longer.)

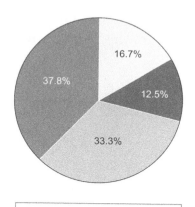

○ Less than one year.
● 1-2 years
◐ 3 years or more
● Other (each 4.2%)
  - 2 1/2 years
  - Still there.
  - 5 months into my first position after separation, no plans of leaving in the near term.
  - 1 year and still in this same position.
  - 7 years
  - I'm still in the position - 4 months strong!
  - N/A
  - 10 years
  - No current position. Still on both boards.

How long did you stay in that first position after separation?

And what did they choose to do next? It varied widely, from stepping into full retirement to pursuing full-time employment, and everything in between.

WHAT DO "PEOPLE LIKE US" END UP DOING?

POLL QUESTION

How would you categorize your first step out of government? (pick one)

Of our Interview Subjects, most chose full time employment in some capacity as their first step out of government, although 15% felt prepared to fully retire and did so. The full time workers were spread among corporations, Federally Funded Research and Development Corporations (FFRDC), or took on Independent Consulting or other self-employment.

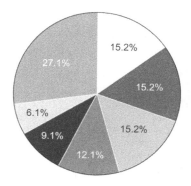

15.2%

27.1%

15.2%

6.1%

15.2%

9.1%

12.1%

○ Sought full-time employment in a corporate capacity for a defense contractor or related industry
● Became self-employed
◐ Fully retired
◑ Sought full-time employment in an industry unrelated to your previous career
● Sought part-time employment
○ Sought full-time work doing staff augmentation in support of your previous employer
◒ Other (each 3 %)
  - Had pre-arranged executive position with a University FFRDC
  - Full-time employment in a private security firm supporting corporate clients
  - Sought full-time employment to give back to USG and capitalize on my unique leadership and experiences
  - Sought full-time work as a US government civilian for a different agency
  - Intended to seek some employment, but wanted to give myself time to explore
  - Sought full-time employment in an industry related to my previous career
  - Combination of seeking PT employment and becoming self-employed
  - Sought full-time employment at a nonprofit associated w/ the IC, DoD, & DHS
  - Taking time for elder care/child care; Advisory Board positions

How would you categorize your first step out of government?

Those separating from Federal Government service often differ from the general population in terms of their professional motivations and drivers. They tend to be strongly motivated by patriotism and service and employer mission, and generally less driven by financial gain. These drivers can influence the types of work that "people like us" choose to pursue after separation from the Federal Government. The majority of the survey respondents chose to stay close to the Federal Government services sector as a first step out of the Federal Government, as either an independent contractor or an industrial contractor. It feels more comfortable than diving into something completely unrelated. It gives the jobseeker a sense that they can continue to serve their country in a support capacity, and it often allows people to leverage clearances to financial advantage. Federal Government contractors are eager to hire those who already have clearances, since they do not have the ability to clear workers without the sponsorship of their Federal Government partner. Of our Interview Subjects who chose to continue working, only 12.5% sought onward employment in a sector unrelated to their previous employment.

CONSIDERING YOUR OPTIONS

There are many possible paths to choose following your separation from government service. A big consideration is whether you would like to fully retire or continue working. Those who chose to fully retire at the end of their government service did so after careful consideration of their finances, and generally did so because the most important thing to them was spending time with family and travel. None of these Interview Subjects had any regrets about that decision. Their perspective was, "life is short, so enjoy it while you can". Those who elected to continue working were divided into part-time and full-time. Those decisions were often financially driven, although personal fulfillment and the need to stay active and engaged also played a role.

Full Retirement

Fifteen percent of our Interview Subjects stated that they went immediately from full-time government employment to full retirement. Those respondents who elected to fully retire immediately cited good financial planning as key to assuring them that they could support themselves for the long haul. Quality of life and family considerations were a big factor in those decisions.

 I had no second thoughts about the decision to fully retire. In fact, I am very thankful now, because six years after I retired, my husband passed away very unexpectedly. I am so thankful we had the years from retirement until then to enjoy our time together. You never know what the future will bring you—don't ever count on forever!

> My husband and I both saw too many people work well into their 60s or 70s only to either develop serious health issues or die fairly soon after retirement. We also saw people struggling with working full time and trying to care for elderly parents or struggling to be available to their children and grandchildren. We did not want to be in these situations. We also wanted to travel, so we made the decision to retire as soon as we were eligible at age 55. We made this decision in our mid-40s and then took steps to prepare financially to be able to do this.

> I was counting the days until I was eligible to retire. I found it very stressful to go into work every day, so reviewed my finances and realized I could probably live on a pension.

> I can finally enjoy being totally relaxed, and having a feeling that the world is my oyster. I can create a new life, one that has meaning, giving back and learning new things. It is exciting.

If you are not prepared to fully retire for whatever reason, there are many options for continuing paid employment. Many are attracted to the idea of working part time and pursuing personal interests part time. Others feel driven to continue working full time for financial or personal fulfillment reasons. Our Interview Subjects' experiences covered the range of options in their discussion of the employment possibilities.

Part-Time Employment

If you wish to take a corporate job, particularly in support of the government services sector, opportunities available to work part time straight-away are limited. Many separating government workers end-up working full-time in a related industry to start, and then scaling back their work hours to part-time once their employer is familiar with their work and sees value to a lightened work schedule.

Working outside the government services sector provides a broader range of work schedule possibilities, including part time. Industries outside of government services tend to be less concerned with filling bill-able hours to the government customer, which generally wants full-time support from everyone.

Twelve percent of our Interview Subjects sought part-time employ-ment at separation. This was broken down into those who wanted to work part time for existing organizations (9.4%), and those who decided to be part-time self-employed (3.1%).

Many of our Interview Subjects ended-up in part-time work situations (often self-employed) following a period of full-time employment. This sort of "phased exit" is very common.

Of those who exited directly to part-time work, here is what they had to say:

Corporate part-time:

 I hit my 35-year mark with government, which felt significant. I had accomplished what I wanted to, and wanted more flexibility with my time since my husband had already been retired for about a year.

Self-employed part time:

 I had no marketable skills in the field I wanted to enter. I spent two years building an expertise and a product.

Full-Time Employment:

The majority of our 33 Panel members sought full-time employment following separation. This consisted of several variations: defense contracting, working in an unrelated industry, working with a University Federally Funded Research and Development Corporation (FFRDC), private security work, working for another government organization as a staff employee, returning to the same organization as an Industrial or Independent Contractor, or working full time in a related industry.

Industries supporting the government sector seek to hire former Federal Government employees for several reasons. Corporations are looking for your connections back into government, and also for your security clearance. These corporations see a short window of opportunity to leverage your access (3–4 years), after which, your contacts and insider knowledge will be considered stale. The first years out of government are therefore often the most lucrative for a recent retiree who wants to work full time. Industry wants you for your understanding of the technical gaps and needs inside government, and also for your contacts. Often, however, after a government retiree has been in industry for a few years, they can scale back on their hours and work part time and/or work remotely from home.

FULL-TIME OPTIONS

As previously discussed, for a variety of reasons, some who leave government elect to pursue a second, full-time career. This could mean continuing in government employment in some capacity, or working in support of the government in the private sector, or pursuing something entirely different. Most transitions out of government tend to be multi-phased, with few people staying in their first post-retirement position for longer than a year or two. In my case, a sequence of valuable private sector experiences provided a "gradual weaning" away from the IC, which made it possible to stay within my comfort zone until I could learn the nuances of a new business area sufficiently.

Let's look at some of the full-time second career options available to you:

Continuing to Support the Government

There are several ways that you can return to support the government post-separation. Here are some of the possibilities:

1. Blue-to-Green Badge: Becoming a contractor for an *Industrial* Contracting company

2. Blue-to-Blue Badge: Becoming a government staffer at the same or another agency

3. Blue-to-Brown Badge: Becoming self-employed as an *Independent* Contractor or consultant to provide services back to the government

Let's evaluate these options:

BLUE-TO-GREEN BADGE

Government Staff Employee to Government Industrial Contractor: There are positives and negatives to going blue-to-green. Here are the advantages and disadvantages.

Advantages

You can leverage your security clearances for financial gain. A TS/SCI clearance with poly enhances your value to a corporation by $10,000-$15,000. Make sure that you get an appropriate signing bonus for the security clearance that you bring where possible. It is very difficult for a company to get new resources cleared, so they are very eager to hire people who bring clearances with them. This is an important card you hold if you want to stay in the Defense and Intelligence services sector.

Companies themselves have no ability to get someone cleared. A government office that owns a contract must sponsor (and pay for) any new clearances for people staffing that contract. Because companies cannot get people cleared on their own, and because government customers are reluctant to pay for new clearances, those who come out of government with existing clearances are in very high demand.

Federal Government contracting tends to pay decent base salaries with additional, sometimes significant, bonus opportunities. They also provide excellent benefits, particularly if you are also drawing a government pension on top of your industry salary. The ability to have a 401(k) with matching employer contributions, profit sharing, equity, and employee stock purchase plans make government contracting an attractive option, particularly for those retiring from government service who still have kids to put through college.

> In my first year in my first job with an industrial contractor, I was given a performance bonus that was big enough to go out and purchase a brand-new car with cash. I was stunned (for a variety of reasons).

Leverage past skills. Do you have subject matter expertise or technical skills that are best used by the government? Are you adept at manipulating specific databases or creating/using specific technologies that are unique to your agency? Do you have training experience inside government that you would like to continue use to help the next generation? Do you clearly want to use these skills in your next job? In this case, going from blue-to-green might be a very good fit for you.

Staying in a familiar/comfortable environment may make transitions easier. Returning to your previous employer as a contractor in some capacity is one option that provides the benefit of seeing old friends and focusing on the same or a similar mission, often with less responsibility and no management hassles. Avoiding a steep learning curve can make the career transition simpler and less stressful.

Government contracting companies value your perspective on their client: Government retirees are generally treated with respect and deference by their private sector colleagues. This can help your sense of well-being.

Disadvantages

If you pursue Staff Augmentation work, understand its downsides. More than anything else, the defense contracting industry is looking to put "butts in seats" with staff augmentation work. You need to think hard about whether or not it will be personally satisfying enough to go back in to the government work space to do the same or similar job to the one you are leaving (with none of the authority and none of the responsibility). Ask yourself the hard questions. Are you okay with being just the expendable "hired help"? Are you comfortable having zero decision-making authority? Are you okay with lack of job security?

Loss of influence and respect can feel demeaning. Once you have a green badge, you will be treated differently. You are no longer an insider.

There are meetings that you will be excluded from. Government staffers, even your good friends, need to be mindful of how they are seen with you. They must be very careful to avoid any perception of bias toward you or your company. You may also encounter staffers who will treat you with disdain, suspicion, or disrespect. It's real. And it hurts.

Less long-term stability/job security. Government contracts are subject to re-compete every 2–10 years and are also subject to continuing-resolution funding. If you opt to take a position doing staff augmentation work, be sure to know when your contract is scheduled to be re-competed so that you do not join an effort that your company then loses a few months down the road.

Being a contractor is higher-risk. You will no longer be considered "essential personnel" in emergency situations or budget reduction exercises or fiscal year-end continuing resolutions or budget freezes. You may be subject to furlough while your staff colleagues continue to work. In furlough or work stoppage situations, most companies do not have the financial ability to pay your salary from their overhead. If you are no longer billable on a contract, you risk loss of your income with no option to recover it.

Understand what it means to sign a "contingent offer". Signing a contingent contract with a company enables your prospective employer to use your name and resume in a proposal in their bid for a contract. It does not mean that they actually have the work or that you will ever have a job. (It means that if they eventually win the work, you can have the position that they bid you on.) Be realistic about the company's chances of winning the contract. Presenting resumés of former staff employees helps a company appear to the government customer as able to bring highly credible, qualified staff to the contract. This improves their chances of winning the work; however, contract proposals are drafted many months before a contract is submitted and eventually awarded. Given the tendency toward award protests, it could be years before the contract is finally awarded and work begins. The contingent offer does not lock you in to work for this company in this job. You should be proactive in pursuing other opportunities in parallel to your contingency offer. Frankly, your chances of ending up in this actual job are very small.

If you pursue a position in corporate overhead (working inside the company doing a corporate function, not being directly billed on contract to a customer), it also has some negatives.

Defense contractors want you for your contact list. Defense contracting is all about developing new business. Whether you are employed in a business development role or some sort of technical or advisory role, Defense Contractors mostly want you for your contacts. They want to be able to leverage your personal relationships to get a competitive edge in pursuing additional work. Are you comfortable being used in this manner? Would you be comfortable knocking on an old colleague's door to learn about their needs and trying to sell them some new capability?

Understand the stark differences between what motivates government and what drives business. Business is all about meeting revenue and profit targets. Period. It is all about Profit and Loss. Our previous career was all about Mission and National Security. While businesses tout being there to support their customers' patriotic missions, they cannot continue to exist without remaining profitable through repeat and new revenue opportunities while also meeting owners/shareholder/market expectations. This contrast between your past employer and your new employer's values and motivations can be uncomfortable for former government employees.

. . .

All business decisions must factor-in the corporate bottom line. You must become accustomed to making business decisions based almost exclusively on profit and loss. It is not always about what is best for the government customer. Business strategy often depends upon getting your foot in the door, and then selling additional capabilities, or up-selling what you currently providing. Be sure to take an objective look at what companies might want from you.

BLUE-TO-BLUE BADGE

Most often, blue-to-blue agency-switchers are former Military who can retire after 20 years of service, transitioning to another full-time government civilian/staff position, either within DoD or with another government agency).

There are advantages and disadvantages to going blue-to-blue:

Positives

- **Continuity of service** time counts toward retirement benefits (In some cases, the clock starts over, and you may be eligible for two retirements).
- **Benefits retention** opportunity to retain excellent retirement programs and health insurance coverage.
- **Broadening your skillset** and professional network on familiar territory.
- **Continuity** in terms of your professional associations.
- **Continued fulfillment with mission focus** (not to be underestimated!)
- Staying within your professional **comfort zone.**
- **Job stability** in terms of firing compared with private sector.

I *can* still make significant contributions to national security *in a new capacity*.

Negatives

 Getting used to a **new organizational culture** and working as a civilian **without the rank and authority** my military position provided.

 I sometimes **miss the gravitas and authority that military rank provided**.

Be sure you have a clear understanding of how your pension and other benefits might be impacted by going blue-to-blue. It may not always be advantageous.

BLUE -TO-BROWN BADGE

"Brown Badgers" are generally Government Staff who have become self-employed in support of the government.

Advantages

- Learning to set up your own company can be **refreshing and reinvigorating.**
- There is **much to learn**. It can be intellectually stimulating.
- Potentially an opportunity to **"make a difference" in another way.**
- Often fast-paced and focused on **innovation.**
- Can provide **greater earning potential, particularly if your aim is to grow, then sell a business.**

- Can be **fulfilling personally, if the new work is for a cause that you deeply believe in.**
- Private sector organizations often use different **business tools and best practices**, which have a learning curve, but they are often more **efficient** than government.

Disadvantages

- **You will need to market/sell your capability**. For many of us this is uncomfortable.

> I feared I would not be able to attract clients and would not know how to do the work required. Those fears were completely realized.

- **More risk/less stability in running your own business**, particularly if you need to gain new skills

> I had no marketable skills in the field I wanted to enter. I spent two years building an expertise and a product.

- In spite of what we might think, **industry does not work 9–5, Monday through Friday.**

> I took on consulting, because that seemed the most obvious skillset I had to offer. I also thought it would allow me to control my time, so I could finally plan a weekend with family or friends. I quickly learned that clients do not respect weekends or evenings and that I was getting client service requests on Friday afternoon, due on Saturday.

- The **start-up costs and effort needed to establish a business can be considerable.**

> I had to learn how to invoice clients, rent furniture, account for expenses, etc. Again—not hard, but that "back office work" takes time.

- It can be also hard to articulate your **transferrable skills** from the government sector.

> I had been doing one thing for so long. I was good at it. I didn't know how to do anything else. Nor did I know how to sell our unique and odd espionage skills on the outside. The fears were realized in that everyone I met respected the CIA and seemed to believe it was important work, but nobody really understands what we do nor can they envision what kind of work we can do in the private sector.

Tips for Going Out on Your Own:

√ Understand the need for reporting and remitting required withholdings at the Federal and State/Local level, e.g. quarterly estimated taxes.

√ Consider the pros and cons of setting your own schedule.

√ It could be very satisfying to build something from the ground up.

√ The learning curve can be steep in starting up a business.

. . .

√ Clearly understand the need to separate business and personal assets.

CHANGING FIELDS ENTIRELY

BLUE-BADGE TO NO BADGE

A "Field Changer", in the context of this book, is a Federal Government employee who becomes self-employed or works for an established employer in a completely unrelated industry, NGO, or nonprofit.

Very few of our Interview Subjects who chose to return to full-time employment opted to change fields entirely and work outside of the Federal Government services sector. Several have ended-up working outside the IC, however, after a series of positions serving the government in some capacity. Several others changed fields and are working on a part-time basis.

Advantages

- A **clean break** to something completely different can be refreshing and reinvigorating.
- **Learning new things is great for intellectual stimulation.**
- Potentially an opportunity to **"make a difference"** in another way.
- Often fast paced and focused on **innovation.**
- Can provide **greater earning potential** (but not always).
- Can be **fulfilling personally if new work is for a cause you deeply believe in.**
- These organizations often use different **business tools and best practices**, which have a learning curve, but which are often more **efficient** than government.

Disadvantages

- Can have more **risk**/less stability.
- **The learning curve can be quite steep.**
- You can **miss** previous work **relationships and the mission** of your government employer.
- Potentially harder to articulate **transferrable skills** from the government sector to the new organization.

WORKSHEET 6

AMBITION INDICATORS

An important conversation with yourself and your life partner should be about your level of career ambition going forward into the next phase of your life. Federal Government employees tend to be high achievers, both in their careers and in their personal lives.

What role will professional ambition play in the next stage of your life? For example, how important is a prestigious job title to you after separating from the Federal Government? Be very honest here. For many in the Intelligence, Foreign Affairs, National Security or Military Community, their title has represented a big part of "who they are".

These are particularly important questions for individuals leaving government service, many of whom have worn their title/rank on their sleeve (literally) for their entire career, and whose social and professional opportunities and status have been defined by their professional grade or rank or title for most of their lives.

Ask yourself these questions:

Do you want another high-powered, high-impact, full-time career position? If so, why?

What is it about that high-powered life that is appealing to you? Is it the prestige? The money? The mission? The ability to control big budgets and make big strategic decisions? The comradery of being on a leadership team? Try to identify your own motivation. Write it down.

How important will it be for you to have a big job title in your next job? Why or why not?

Do you truly want a "second career" where your intent is to climb the corporate ladder to become a senior corporate executive? What would that look like for you, immediately upon separation? In two years? In five years? In 10 years?

Do you have a realistic view of what that senior business executive life entails? (Corporate leaders cannot leave their work at the office or behind in a vault. They are expected to be fully accessible and available to respond 24/7, including weekends and often to include time on vacation.)

Are you interested in returning to your old workplace doing a similar job without the management responsibilities? What's appealing about that option? What's not very appealing about that option?

Do you want to gradually "fade away" to fully retired status? How gradually? Can you put that "fade" on a timeline with the types of work that you envision pursuing immediately upon separation, in two years, in five years, in 10 years.

Two-year plan/position -

Five-year plan/position -

10-year plan/position —

In your first step out of the Federal Government, how far removed do you want to be from the Intelligence, Foreign Affairs, National Security or Military Community? Why?

WORKSHEET 7

DEVELOPING YOUR OWN VISION FOR THE FUTURE

Looking Forward

Consider the following questions as you begin to develop your own vision for your future life.

How would you like to spend your "second adulthood"? Can you put it into words?

What would you still like to learn?

What is meaningful to you?

What do you want your legacy to be?

How do you want to be remembered?

What is still on your "bucket list"?

What are your personal dreams?

How do you want your next job to fit into the future that you want to create for yourself and your loved ones?

Brainstorming new ideas; leaving a legacy

What do you know about yourself that nobody else does?

I want to help people solve_____ (issue or problem).

What have you always been attracted to? What is "calling" you?

What have you been wondering about for many years?
(I always found _____ interesting.)

Do you have a hobby that you have considered turning into your next career?

What section of the bookstore are you always drawn toward?
(I am intrigued by_____)

What have you always dreamed of?

It would be great if I could_____.

WORKSHEET 8

BEYOND YOUR GOVERNMENT CAREER,
WHAT DO YOU WANT TO BE REMEMBERED FOR?

Consider your legacy. While it can seem like a morbid topic, your pre-transition phase might be the perfect time to think about what you consider to be a "life well-lived". Think about your complete life, not just the years when you worked for the government. When your life is over, what will you have accomplished, not only as a public servant, but also in your post-separation career and/or personal life?

Thinking through these questions can help you identify areas where you still feel unfulfilled. This can lead to brainstorming new ways that you can achieve those goals and dreams that still remain on your "bucket list".

Write your own obituary and include the following:

Who did you work for (the Federal Government, and after retiring from government service)?

What did you accomplish academically?

What did you accomplish in your life?

What do you consider your most significant personal accomplishments in your life?

What personal and professional goals did you meet or exceed?

What sacrifices did you make in order to help/develop others?

What dreams did you accomplish?

What was your greatest career achievement?

What was your greatest life achievement?

How would you like to be remembered by your family? By your friends? By your former colleagues? By acquaintances?

WORKSHEET 9

MELDING YOUR PERSONAL AND PROFESSIONAL GOALS

At this stage of your life, it is time to consider how you define your own Personal Success and your own Professional Success. Perhaps you already achieved what you consider to be adequate professional success and are able to step off the professional merry-go-round and move forward with personal fulfillment. Maybe you still have more that you want to prove to yourself and achieve professionally.

This exercise is designed to help you consider your own personal life goals, values and priorities as well as your professional ones. Then you can evaluate how the personal goals, values, and priorities rank and integrate with the professional ones.

<u>GOALS QUESTIONS</u>

Personal

Consider these questions as you look to balance your personal goals and priorities with your professional ones in the next stage of your life.

What is your personal definition of success as a whole person? (e.g., "I would consider my life personally successful if I could....")

What are your top 3 personal lifestyle goals (in priority order)? (e.g., "My goal is to live in house on the beach that I own free and clear."

1.

2.

3.

What are your top 3 dreams/ultimate life goals going forward (in priority order)? (e.g., My dream is for my spouse and me to take a round-the-world trip while we still have our health.)

1.

2.

3.

Professional

What is your professional definition of success? (e.g., I would consider myself profes-sionally successful if I....)

If you would like to continue to work, what are your 2-year career goals?

1.

2.

3.

If you would like to continue to work beyond 2 years, what are your 5- and 10-year career goals?

1.

2.

3.

Now let's evaluate how you might balance your future lifestyle goals with your future professional goals in the next stage of your life. Ask yourself these questions:

How do my stated professional goals (above) help to facilitate/enable the achievement of my stated personal definition of success? How will my stated career goals (above) help me to achieve the lifestyle that I dream of for myself and my family?

How will my career goals above help me to achieve my dreams/life goals?

How could my career goals actually prevent me from having time to pursue my dreams/life goals?

Will a career always be necessary for me in order to achieve my other life goals? Does work still figure prominently in my definition of success? Why or why not?

As you consider your career transition, do you still want to "live to work" (as most high achievers have always done), or would you prefer now to downshift and "work to live" (if you work at all)?

Many struggle with career transition because they miss the feeling of being needed at work. How can you smoothly shift your work/life priorities without feeling lost? Are there other things that you can do in your new life to satisfy your intrinsic need to feel needed?

Make a plan. Are there specific steps you need to take to ensure that you can reach your top personal and professional goals listed above? Can you put these steps on a timeline?

STEPS TO TAKE

Planned Completion Date:_____

1.

2.

3.

4.

WORKSHEET 10

UNDERSTANDING YOUR OWN PERSONAL
AND PROFESSIONAL VALUES

It is well understood that the majority of employees who leave an organization do so due to lack of connection with the organization's mission, the work environment or culture/core values, or as a result of a poor working relationship with a direct manager. Many people end-up unhappy in a job because the organization's values or a supervisor's values are not in alignment with their own. The impact of such a misalignment should not be under-estimated. A career transition is an excellent opportunity to reflect upon your individual values—both life values and career values. This exercise is designed to help you think about what sort of organization you might like to work for based upon your own set of personal and career values.

VALUES EXERCISE

(Reprinted with permission of the author, Diane Hudson, Professional Association of Resumé Writers and Career Coaches, Certified Professional Career Coach Program Director © 2016)

What are your Top 5 Life Values? (example: free time for grandchildren)

1.

2.

3.

4.

5.

What are your Top 5 Career Values? (example: a work environment that provides structure)

1.

2.

3.

4.

5.

Value Requirements & Priorities (List your Top 6 values from both boxes above, then place them in order of priority)

   A.

   B.

   C.

   D.

E.

F.

What things do you NOT value in your work? - What will quickly burn you out? (example: a micromanager boss; working in crowded, shared spaces, etc.)

1.

2.

3.

4.

5.

Values Comparison

Required in My Career

1.

2.

3.

4.

5.

Not Required in My Career

1.

2.

3.

4.

5.

6.

As you begin to evaluate organizations and positions that you may wish to consider for future employment, refer back to this values sheet and think about how that new organization/position fits (or doesn't fit) with your stated set of values.

PART IV

THE MECHANICS OF LEAVING

7

UNDERSTANDING YOUR MARKETABLE SKILL SETS

Before you draft any sort of resumé, this is the right time for self-assessment. Self-assessment can be a challenging and uncomfortable process, and it is often easier/more comfortable to skip this step and just start banging out resumés.

NOTE: THE RESUMÉ DOES NOT COME FIRST!

This chapter will help you think through what specific skills and attributes you have to offer to a future employer. This is the prelude to writing a resumé. Set aside a few hours in a quiet place for self-reflection. Here's how our respondents went about deciding what their marketable skills were:

ASSESSING YOUR SKILLS

POLL QUESTION

How did you identify your most marketable external skills?

Interview Subjects found the process of actually writing a resume helpful in terms of assessing their individual skills. Many also used the advice of mentors to help them translate their skills into corporate jargon. Here are their most relevant comments.

Resumé Writing

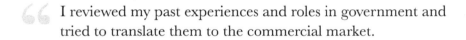 I reviewed my past experiences and roles in government and tried to translate them to the commercial market.

Through the process of talking with others and asking their views and thinking about what to highlight on my resumé. Writing the resumé, in itself, was an activity of self-reflection.

This was probably the most difficult step for me, in large part because I did not go the contractor route. First, I found a way to express what I did in government in business terms. For example, a corporate board provides oversight for a company and during interviews I speak about my experience with Congressional oversight. Second, the CIA taught me how to be a critical thinker, which increasingly is a lost art. This means as a board member I can ask thoughtful questions without being an expert on a subject. Critical thinking also helps me provide credible oversight on three areas—

cybersecurity, financial threats, and global risk—that are in my wheelhouse. Finally, I determined that mission-focus is still important to me. As a result, I am focusing on critical infrastructure in my search for additional board service.

Mentor Advice

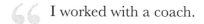 I worked with a coach.

It took time, effort and self-kindness. I started looking at what I love to do and selling those things—people bought them and have referred me to others who buy them.

USE OF ASSESSMENTS

POLL QUESTION

Did you take any (commercially available) skills or behavioral assessments as part of your career transition process? If so, which ones?

Although only a few of our Interview Subjects used assessments to help them define their skills, these tools can be very useful. Assessments can provide excellent language to help you describe your specific behavioral and communication style in the workplace. When a hiring manager looks to add someone to their work team, they will want to be able to envision how that applicant might fit-in with existing team members. The manager will want someone who complements existing personalities and skills (but doesn't duplicate attributes already held by team members), because the most effective workplace has employees with differing skills, abilities, communication styles, and behavioral styles.

Interview Subjects listed the following assessments as having been helpful:

- StrengthsFinder
- Myers Briggs
- Highlands Ability Battery
- DISC Motivators and Values Assessment
- DISC Self-Assessment
- Hogan
- Leadership Circle
- Strong Invest Inventory
- VIA
- EQ-I

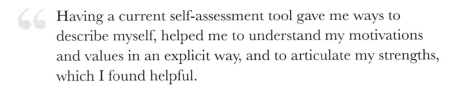

Having a current self-assessment tool gave me ways to describe myself, helped me to understand my motivations and values in an explicit way, and to articulate my strengths, which I found helpful.

I had been through most of the successive senior executive leadership courses at NGA and in the IC. In each of these, there were various personal and '360 degree' assessments, including Myers-Briggs, etc. I always found value in these— particularly in understanding the delta between how I saw myself and how others saw me.

POLL QUESTION

Did your own assessment of your marketable skills prove accurate, or did you need to revamp your value proposition over time?

Respondents were fairly evenly split on whether or not they understood their marketable skills upon separation. Some struggled to identify their marketable skills at first and necessarily changed how they marketed themselves over time as they learned more about the job market. Others (the majority) believed they had a good understanding of their marketable skills and how those skills fit a company's needs. We talk more about value propositions in Chapter 9 of this book.

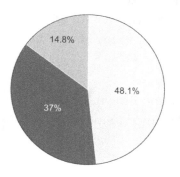

○ At the time of separation I had a good understanding of my marketable skills and how they fit a company's needs.

● I struggled to identify my specific marketable skills and needed to modify how I marketed myself over time.

○ Other (each 3.7%)

   - Somewhere in between the two above choices. I had a good understanding of my marketable skills but did need to work on how I presented myself and articulated my skills as a potential fit.

   - I can't recall such an assessment.

   - I had no marketable skills in the field I wanted to enter. I spent two years building an expertise and a product.

   - A variation on choice #1 above

Did your own assessment of your marketable skills prove accurate or did you need to revamp your value proposition?

POLL QUESTION

Did you take additional training after separation to prepare for your next career phase? What additional training did you take? Why did you feel that you needed additional training?

Some Interview Subjects believed that they needed to acquire additional skills and tools after separation in order to be competitive in their next field. Sometimes these were skills that they would not have been able to obtain while in government service. In this instance, the additional skills were to build professional credibility in a new field, or to fill a real or perceived skill gap to be on par with private sector colleagues.

66 The training and certifications I pursued post-transition - leadership, team, and conflict coaching, facilitation, design thinking, and DiSC and team assessments - were to give me an anchor for my interests and credibility in my chosen new profession.

66 I became a certified facilitator for Brené Brown. I have always been a fan of her work and wanted to meet her. It has paid off immensely.

66 I pursued an Instructional Systems Design certification to enhance my teaching resumé

66 I've taken some online classes, mainly through the International Coaching Federation, to boost my coaching credentials and learn business basics.

66 I needed training in how to use CRM (contact relationship management) tools to support my company.

> I pursued a PMP (Project Management Professional) certification, which I found to be extremely difficult for someone without a business background.

> I needed to get comfortable with current commercial technology (how to use a laptop, multiple business function Apps on a smartphone, iPad, Conference calls, spreadsheets, Word, etc.)

> I've taken some online classes, mainly through the International Coaching Federation, to boost my coaching credentials and learn business basics.

POLL QUESTION

Were there additional skills or certifications you wish you had obtained/mastered while still a government employee in preparation for your next step?

Many of the Interview Subjects left government and moved into roles with defense contracting firms. Therefore, it is not surprising that a number of Interview Subjects wished they had greater exposure to project management, program management, and the contract management process. This was particularly noted by individuals who came out of career fields where contracts were awarded and managed by people in other parts of their government organizations. Some of the non-military respondents also mentioned lacking skills in PowerPoint.

> I wish I had understood more about the contracting process. People who work in Operations have little or no exposure to contract management, the Request for Proposal (RFP) process, contract reviews, etc. It would also have been useful

to become a Contracting Officer's Technical Representative (COTR).

66 I would like to have gotten certified in facilitation, and/or gotten an instructor certification.

66 I wish I had developed a better understanding of cloud-based technologies and Excel, Powerpoint, Sharepoint.

66 Program Management.

66 I believe a ASIS-Certified Protection Professional certification would have been useful.

66 Cyber-security credentials would have been worthwhile.

66 Perhaps a coaching certificate.

66 My one (little) regret from my government career—not taking advantage of more training opportunities that were available, both internal (like Harvard negotiation training) and external (funding for education, such as towards an MBA or an advanced degree in Industrial Organizational Psychology, or Organizational Development).

BUT *WE* ARE SPECIAL!
We didn't have ordinary careers. What are OUR most marketable skills?

Having a credible list of skills from our unique career fields is very valuable as you begin to think about how to market yourself. In this study, individuals with backgrounds in Intelligence, Foreign Affairs, National Security and the Military were asked what they believe to be their 10 most marketable skills based upon their own subsequent private sector work experiences. Their responses were many and varied. However, the skills they cited can be put into 5 key skill areas. These are:

- Leadership and Teamwork,
- Analytics and Problem-solving,
- Communication,
- Soft skills/people skills,
- Specific Technical Expertise.

The skill lists below can be very useful as you prepare for interviews, or as you think about what to emphasize in a resumé or job application.

POLL QUESTION

What do you believe are the 10 most marketable skills in the private sector for someone coming out of the IC/government to highlight?

Leadership and Teamwork

The most effective way to demonstrate your leadership, teamwork, and professionalism to a prospective employer is to have some very short, candid examples/stories prepared to demonstrate your skills in key areas.

Employers will be looking for leaders who can work with a team to develop a set of alternatives to solve a problem, while also reducing/mitigating risks for the organization. These stories will be most impactful if they can demonstrate future benefit to an organization, such as helping to achieve cost-savings, increase in profitability, building/repairing key partnerships, winning/securing additional key business, or solving a critical problem.

In this category, the respondents listed the following skills as most marketable from their perspective:

- Demonstrated proven leadership ability
- Institutional leadership (versus small-team leadership)
- Managing change
- Knowing how bureaucracies work and how to work within/around them
- Understanding the mission faster than anyone else and how to stay focused on it
- Understanding of leadership in an organization
- Ability to manage and lead employees
- Leadership and management (depending on the levels you achieved in government)
- Understanding and ability to execute in the broader context of the national security enterprise
- Critical decision-making skills
- Willingness to take calculated risks
- Risk identification
- Risk mitigation
- Risk management
- Crisis management
- Working with others/teamwork
- Teaming skills
- Team-building
- Collaboration
- Coordination

Some additional leadership skills might include the following:

- Accuracy
- Attention to detail
- Brainstorming
- Consistently meeting deadlines
- Creative thinking
- Detail orientation
- Determination
- Drawing consensus on group goals
- Effectively managing multiple projects simultaneously
- Facilitating productive meetings
- Flexibility
- Focus
- Forecasting
- High achievement
- Managing to a bottom line
- Managing difficult people
- Mentoring staff
- Motivating staff
- Organizational skills
- Prediction
- Professional demeanor
- Profit and loss
- Providing constructive criticism
- Project design
- Project planning
- Recovering quickly from setbacks
- Respectful
- Responsible
- Results-driven
- Resolving conflicts
- Self-motivated
- Strategic planning

- Strong work ethic
- Success-driven
- Tact and diplomacy
- Time management

Analytics and Problem Solving

In your government career, you have helped to solve global, national, regional, and local problems. Every organization needs active problem-solvers. These are highly marketable skills.

Analytic Skills refer to your ability to collect and analyze information, problem-solve, and make decisions. Many people in the Intelligence Community are involved in conducting analysis and doing analytics. These jobs (and many others in the IC) require this kind of critical thinking on some level. An employee's analytic strength can help solve a company's problems and increase its productivity. Showing the employer that you can gather and analyze information, resolve problems, and make decisions will enhance your candidacy.

Be prepared to provide short, high-impact, unclassified examples of your analytic and problem-solving abilities in an interview situation.

• **Some Analytics examples from our careers**: Diagnosing difficulties in a critical bilateral partnership, identifying causes for a technical failure, recognizing invalid research models.

• **Some Problem Solving examples from our careers:** Evaluating alternative strategies for solving a technical problem, proposing diplomatic solutions to a bilateral conflict, selecting essential and non-essential employees during a budget-driven furlough or crisis situation, troubleshooting computer malfunctions.

The Interview Subjects listed their own analytic and problem-solving skills as follows:

Analytics and Problem Solving: In this category, the Interview Subjects listed the following skills as most marketable from their perspective:

- Critical thinking
- Analytic skills—gathering info, considering sourcing and gaps, and drawing conclusions
- Assessment
- Deep reading and study of all available materials
- Ability to interpret big events overseas, applying these skills to a broader set of issues
- Ability to gather data and information, synthesize/distill it, and think critically, and to communicate the outcome to a leader who must make a decision or take action
- Problem solving, including in situations where there are not clear right and wrong answers
- Financial analysis skills

Other analytic and problem-solving skills from the public sector might include:

- Assessing needs and preferences
- Assessing outcomes
- Assessing risk
- Benchmarking
- Case analysis
- Causal analysis
- Comparative analysis
- Complex problem solving
- Correlation
- Creative thinking
- Critical thinking
- Data gathering and analysis
- Decision-making

- Deductive reasoning
- Deep research
- Designing innovative products
- Data analytics
- Data mining
- Diagnostics
- Efficiency
- Evaluative analysis
- Fact-finding
- Good judgment
- Historical analysis
- Innovation
- Judgment
- Listening
- Logical thinking
- Open mindedness
- Policy analysis
- Predictive analytics
- Prioritization
- Process analysis
- Return on investment analysis
- Scenario analysis
- Statistical analysis
- Understanding hidden needs

Communication

Most professionals coming out of the Intelligence Community, Foreign Affairs, the Military, or National Security jobs tend to be strong writers and effective oral communicators. These communication skills are critical for almost any private sector job. Whether you are giving a presentation, talking on the phone to a client, or emailing a colleague, you need to be able to communicate effectively and appropriately. As you might expect, your communication skills will be evaluated in the written materials you use to apply for a job. A hiring manager will also focus on how well you handle the interview and communicate with the people you meet during the hiring process. Employers will also want to see that you can effectively engage with people, listen, respond to concerns, and demonstrate empathy for others. These interpersonal skills are particularly important in jobs that involve customer service or working on a team. The interview provides the best means for a prospective employer to assess your communication skills. This is the place to demonstrate your friendliness and engaging personality.

In this category, the Interview Subjects listed the following skills as most marketable from their perspective:

- Ability to communicate clearly, concisely and diplomatically, both verbally and in writing
- Compelling speaking/briefing/presentation skills
- Facilitation skills
- Interpersonal skills that enable effective teamwork
- Ability to maintain and grow a thriving, diverse professional network

Some additional communication skills from your government experience might include:

- Business storytelling
- Calming customers in high-stakes situations
- Clearly conveying features and benefits of products/services
- Composing engaging written (and interactive) products for consumers
- Establishing credibility and drawing followers as a Subject Matter Expert
- Explaining implications
- Likeability

- Negotiation skills
- Nonverbal communication
- Persuasion skills
- Technical-writing abilities
- Value propositions

Management and Delivery Skills

In private industry, management and delivery skills relate to planning, organizing, coordinating, directing, leadership, and oversight of an area or a product. If interested in working in the field of project or program management in your next job, you may wish to consider getting a certification as a Project Management Professional (PMP) from the Project Management Institute. This certification is well-recognized. As a cautionary note, the PMP exam is very challenging for those with no previous business experience or formal business education. PMP "Boot camps" are sometimes available at local community colleges, or can be arranged (and paid for) by your new employer to prepare you to take the exam.

In this category, the Interview Subjects listed the following skills as most marketable from their perspective:

- Project management
- Program management
- People and resource management
- Mission-focus
- Ability to manage priorities
- Time management
- Executing to a budget
- Fiscal management
- Management by objective
- Organizational skills

- We know how to "get shit done"
- Understanding of "how things work"
- Knowledge where to go for answers
- Discipline to work independently but keep seniors apprised (there is much remote work these days).

A partial list of additional Management and Delivery skills from your government service might include:

- Planning
- Communication
- Delegating
- Problem-solving
- Motivating

Soft Skills

While hard skills or technical competencies (see below) concern an employee's ability to do a specific task, soft skills are more about the way in which they do them—how they adapt, collaborate, solve problems, and make decisions. Soft skills are more about behavior and thinking, personal traits, emotional intelligence and cognitive skills. They can also help a person thrive in a variety of roles and industries. Soft skills matter to a hiring manager and are important to emphasize in an interview. This can help you distinguish yourself from other applicants you may be competing with. Describing your soft skills can help the hiring manager to consider how you will fit into the current mix of his/her team.

Behavioral and communication style assessments such as DISC and Myers-Briggs can help you gain perspective (and find language) to describe your own soft skills and attributes that might be highly sought-after.

The Interview Subjects listed the following "Soft skills" as having been marketable for them in their own second careers:

- Strong sense of ethics and high integrity
- Dependability/Reliability
- Responsiveness
- Undeterred by a formidable challenge
- "Can-do" mindset
- Breadth of perspective
- Ability to continuously learn
- Asking the right questions
- Positive attitude
- Ability to make the best of circumstances
- Always looking for lessons learned
- Willing to explore and learn
- High level of initiative
- Self-confidence (there is lots of "fake it 'til you make it" in business)
- Maturity
- Coping with stress
- Strong mission focus and commitment
- Solid judgment
- Ability to think calmly under stress
- Demonstrated commitment to mission
- Ability to learn and grow continually
- Ability to succeed in a variety of environments
- Professional and intellectual flexibility and agility
- Adaptability
- We like to move fast
- Resiliency
- Adept at managing in times of change
- Working with and in a variety of organizations/cultures (particularly true if you held joint-duty assignments)
- Ability to assess and "read" people

- Emotional intelligence
- Understanding of human nature and recruitment
- Ease with people at all levels
- Networking
- Ability to quickly assess situations
- Personal connections; more connections; and more connections
- Extensive list of contacts potentially useful to the employer
- Professional networks
- Working well with a very wide range of personality types
- International experience
- Cultural competency
- Ability to develop diverse relationships and networks
- Global perspective and experience (living or traveling overseas)

Technical Competencies

Hard skills or technical competencies include job-specific specialized knowledge and technical abilities, such as software development, payroll systems, or product expertise. They are teachable and often easier to define and measure than soft skills. For those coming out of the government sector, your technical competencies may or may not be competitive with those coming out of industry. Often industry outpaces government in the area of technical innovation.

In this category, the Interview Subjects listed the following skills and functional knowledge as most marketable from their perspective:

- Comfort with technology
- Counterterrorism skills
- Cyber security (protecting networks, understanding threats)
- Cyber technology
- Budget development

- Metric-based performance management
- Understanding legal compliance requirements
- Investigations-related skills
- Facilities management
- Business continuity experience
- Strategic planning
- Legislative liaison
- Specific government processes (for example, the intelligence planning cycle or security assistance management)
- Understand and be able to execute in the broader context of the national security enterprise
- Government programming budgeting cycles
- Organizational budget processes
- Relevant subject matter expertise
- Intimate knowledge of a particular government organization
- Business development
- Sales
- Operational-planning skills
- Open source analysis
- Persuasive skills
- Understanding corporate jargon ("contract-speak")
- Understanding the Federal Acquisition Regulations (FAR) process and compliance requirements
- Resource management
- Information technology
- Engineering
- Human resources
- Data science
- Long-range planning skills
- Your understanding of the IC and your agency/organization
- Business process improvement skills
- Foreign language skills
- Understanding how the government works
- Substantive knowledge—regional or functional

- Knowledge of government operations
- Technical acumen

Some additional technical skills considered "in-demand" in 2020 might include:

- Blockchain
- Cloud computing
- Analytical reasoning
- Artificial intelligence (AI)
- User Experience (UX) and User Interface (UI) design
- Business analysis
- Marketing
- Sales
- Scientific computing
- Video production

8

DEVELOPING A JOB SEARCH STRATEGY

If you seek onward employment after separating, a job search strategy should be the next step in your career transition journey. As part of your strategy, it is important to factor in your personal and professional values and your motivators, the mission of any future employer, your individual compensation requirements, any specific benefits that you may desire, the team you work with, proximity to home, and whether (or not) the work requires a clearance.

Federal Government employees spend their whole careers driven by a mission to protect and defend the United States and advance its foreign policy. These patriots have special motivations. Unlike the general pool of jobseekers, government employees highly value a job where they can find personal satisfaction from serving the nation and the greater good. While compensation is also a driver for retiring "govies" who seek a second career, our study shows that the level of compensation is generally second to finding work in a place where they can get behind the mission of their next employer.

As you begin to develop your own job search strategy, it is important to consider the reasons why you have done the jobs that you have done in the past. This is getting to the essence of your personal and professional values and motivations.

JOB SEARCH PRIORITIES

POLL QUESTION

What were your top priorities in deciding what to do next (compensation, benefits, title, mission, team, full time/part time, flexible workplace, travel, other)?

Here were the top 6 priorities of our respondents in the next job they sought:

- Mission of the employer
- Compensation
- Proximity to home
- Drawn to work for a specific team
- Part-time options
- Specific benefits (401k, insurance, Personal Time Off, etc.)

Other responses included:

- Job title
- Flexible workplace
- Travel (or lack of travel)
- Leveraging a clearance
- The commute
- Career development
- Transitioning to a nonprofit
- Interesting and exciting work
- Company culture and reputation

FINDING YOUR FIELD

POLL QUESTION

How did you narrow down your initial range of opportunities?

As they began to look at various potential employers and sectors of employment, our Interview Subjects found themselves less motivated by financial incentives, and more interested in landing jobs where they could learn and grow. They also used their network of contacts to help them evaluate the range of opportunities that they were considering.

> I evaluated by opportunity and the excitement of using my skills in a new unique way.

> Defined in priority my preferred types of jobs; defined what I ideally wanted to do and what I was willing to do based on type of job and compensation. Left my mind very open to what I was willing to do.

> I evaluated by industry, skill set, geography, position.

> By doing job interviews and courtesy meetings.

> Looked for a job that interested me versus money. A job that would develop me.

> I spoke to everyone I could think of. Networked.

> The interview process helped me to find the culture that was the best fit for me.

Through discussions with retired colleagues and my own job searches.

YOUR JOB SEARCH STRATEGY – WHAT WORKS BEST?

THIS SHOULD BE YOUR BIGGEST TAKEAWAY FROM THIS BOOK!

Hands-down, the best way to find a new opportunity for former government employees is through NETWORKING!

POLL QUESTION

What job search strategy proved most successful for you? (Professional networking, online postings, joining professional associations, job fairs, job boards, headhunter, career coach, personal connections, other)? Explain what and why.

Almost every single Interview Subject stated that **networking** was the key to obtaining the best-fitting onward employment. This was emphasized over and over. It is particularly important for those separating from the Federal Government, because our network understands our skills and attributes, and can help us translate what we did in government into what we can do on the outside. Our network can also help us understand the nuances of opportunities presented to us. A few Interview Subjects also commented on the value of attending job fairs, particularly events organized by the government employer that allows access to government contractors. Here are the comments of the Interview Subjects on job search strategy:

Professional networking, LinkedIn, talking to anyone on the outside who was willing to meet with me.

Professional networking was the best strategy. I talked with former co-workers and friends. I didn't find the job websites terribly useful...maybe I didn't give them a chance. To me, the job websites were a shot in the dark. For me, I was more comfortable leveraging personal connections.

Personal, professional connections (my 'network') was key for me, as it played a key role in each of my consultancies. I also made use of job fairs, online tools (LinkedIn, job searches), etc., I was generally disappointed with the results. and found the personal network yielded better, more immediate outcomes.

I was amazed how many people would talk with me, would be willing to help me, and were willing to introduce me to others. It was amazing and gratifying, and I am so grateful —and keep in touch with almost every one of those people!

Professional networking, career coach, personal connections. It is really all about who you know. Blindly applying for a position online got me nothing. Word of mouth and having others advocate for you is the way to go.

MORE JOB SEARCH TIPS

POLL QUESTION

What job search strategy tips you would give a colleague who is about to begin an external job search campaign?

" While it is scary and you sometimes doubt that your skills will fit on the outside, you need to make the mental shift and be able to project *confidence* that you bring value added to any prospective new employer. Those people who fail to project their value take longer to land in a new position. Network like crazy.

" Make a list of all the friends and formal colleagues that you know who are on the outside and start letting them know you are available and looking. Get them your resumé and ask them to look it over. You will be surprised how many people are willing to help—and be that person when you get out as well.

" Set up a space and dedicated times for focusing on your career search; make a list of everyone you know, reach out to them, keep track of them, ask them for their help, and who they know; get online and look at LinkedIn, Glassdoor, and best places to work lists; take the time for self-reflection to focus on what you want, your values, and what you like to do; and invest in a career coach, a resumé and bio writer, and someone to help develop your brand.

" First, know what your interests are; second, determine if you want to work for a large corporation or small company; third, attend all the Agency-organized retirement job fairs, and give them your name and take their business cards. If you can purchase some business cards with your name and phone number, and pass them to the various companies, it will make your job search/contact easier, and fourth, network via colleagues and others.

" Network, Network, Network.... Do it now and make contacts during conferences, speaking engagements, professional interactions, educational requirements, etc. and develop a system to stay in touch with those contacts over time. Target those industries and positions that interest you and leverage any network or contact into those that you may have...not just once but repeatedly over time. Be vocal about your plan to retire soon and your openness about discussing possibilities and taking tips. It's not being disloyal. It's commonsense preparation. Understand that it is going to take a significant time expenditure on your part and invest in it. Be realistic about salary expectations and do some math so that you have a ball park of what you need vs. what you want. Finally, understand the myths and fantasies out there. The job is not going to come to you out of the blue and land in your lap. It happens, but not often. You have to work at it. Furthermore, tales of fantastical salary packages are just that...tales. There is a range for different experience levels, positions, locations, and industries. Acquaint yourself with that range and adjust your expectations within it.

 Answer some basic questions before even beginning the search. What are your objectives for this next phase of your life? Are you more comfortable in a big organization or small? How much change are you willing to put up with, and how willing are you to "reinvent" yourself by moving to a completely different profession? What compensation do you need? What are your family's needs?

ORGANIZING YOUR JOB SEARCH

You will quickly discover that your outreach for various job opportunities needs to be systematically tracked by some method. After you submit a number of job applications, or talk with multiple people, they will slowly begin to blur together. At a minimum, you should consider setting up a spreadsheet to track your job search activities. You may wish to set up columns to make notes on the following topics:

- Name of the organization
- Point of contact
- Position applied for (including position number if applicable, and a link to the job posting/description)
- Date applied/date resumé submitted
- Date of personal interview/informational interview
- Dates and content of any follow-up conversations
- Names and positions of other individuals spoken with
- Your notes on organizational "feel"/culture, any specifics on terms, pros and cons based on your discussions to date
- Type of contract (contingent or non-contingent)
- Specific benefits offered
- How will they measure success in the position?

SYSTEM OF ORGANIZATION TO TRACK APPLICATIONS AND RESUMÉS

POLL QUESTION

What system did you use to track resumés sent, responses received, individuals contacted, interviews completed and notes?

As you will see from their responses below, the Interview Subjects' tended to be fairly low-tech in organizing themselves to track their potential employment opportunities. More and more applications and tools are now available, however, to enable better job search tracking.

Excel spreadsheet.

Email folders.

None. I only used indeed.com as I searched for potential jobs.

Lots of sticky notes! Seriously, I had no system and would highly recommend to others to develop even a simple organizational system for a job search.

Spiral notebook.

Home computer, email data base.

I set up a file system with notes, correspondence, and relevant data on each prospective client.

I started a separate gmail account to be used exclusively for business. I dedicated a part of our home to my business and transition activities. I still love hard copies of correspondence, so I created a filing system to keep track of things.

9

WHAT IS MY "VALUE PROPOSITION" TO A PROSPECTIVE EMPLOYER?

The Value Proposition is very important in a job search, because often, there are many (perhaps hundreds of) applicants for an advertised position. Of those applicants, dozens could be similarly qualified. Your Value Statement will be your way of distinguishing yourself from the crowd and making you appear worthy of an interview. To most effectively market yourself to prospective employers, it is important to understand and be able to articulate what differentiates you from the other, equally qualified candidates.

Developing your own Value Statement requires research. If you do not know the answers to these questions, do some market research and reach out to contacts and connections who can help you understand the landscape.

STEPS TO DEVELOPING A VALUE PROPOSITION

(Source: *greatresumesfast.com* – a step-by-step guide to create a value proposition statement for your resumé, by Jessica Holbrook Hernandez)

1. Think about the industry or industries that you would like to break into.

- *Are there particular companies that are leaders in that industry? Who are they?*
- *What are the main challenges and needs facing those industries/companies? What problems do they need to solve?*
- *What do they most value in someone in the role that you are applying for? (What do they value in a prospective employee? How does the position you seek play into solving the organization's biggest challenges?)*
- *What do they most value in someone in the role that you are applying for? (What do they value in a prospective employee? How does the position you seek play into solving the organization's biggest challenges?)*

2. Make the connection between your own professional experiences and your target industry's greatest needs.

- *Consider how your own past accomplishments, successes and experience point to how you can help to solve the employer's greatest problems or needs. Do you have a track record of solving similar challenges?*
- *Can you provide examples of your past professional results in terms of metrics? (Think about numbers you can provide to demonstrate the value you have offered in previous positions -- revenue you generated, time saved, improvements in client satisfaction, increases in efficiency/productivity.) Try to provide specific numbers, metrics and percentages that prove the value that you can offer to help a new employer to solve their biggest challenges. A credible track record from the past in solving similar problems is highly influential in hiring decisions.*

3. Understand your competition. How are your experiences and credentials similar to (or different from) similarly qualified candidates for this positon?

- *Do a SWOT (Strengths, Weaknesses, Opportunities and Threats) analysis on yourself. Use your self-understanding or an assessment tool to document your strengths. Good behavioral and communication style assessment tools include DiSC, MBTI or Strengthsfinder.*
- *Understand how people are competing in your industry: List the decision criteria (explicit and hidden) that hiring managers use in making hiring decisions for this and similar positions. Rank yourself and your likely competitors by these criteria. Look at where you rank well, and craft a Value Proposition from this.*

4. Emphasize your strengths.

- *Think about the answer to: "I should hire this candidate because ..." Include two or three reasons based on your self-analysis. Incorporate numbers or percentages into the sentences.*

Edit until you're able to clearly communicate your value proposition in one to two sentences. Be specific.

VALUE PROPOSITIONS

POLL QUESTION

Did you understand what it meant to develop "value proposition" for a second career?

In conducting this survey, it became clear that our government transition programs do a less-than-effective job of explaining the concept of (and importance of) value propositions and personal branding to those exiting the Federal Government. Only about 1/3 of respondents understood what a Value Proposition was and were able to explain what their own unique value proposition would be to a prospective employer. These numbers are similar-to the general job-seeking population.

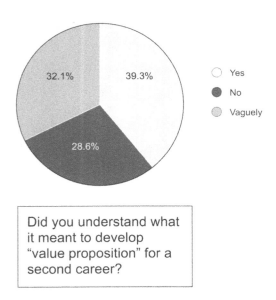

Did you understand what it meant to develop "value proposition" for a second career?

POLL QUESTION

When you left government, were you able to easily articulate what your value proposition would be to a prospective employer?

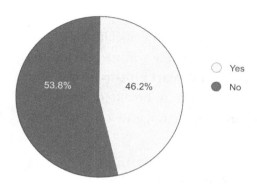

53.8%   46.2%

○ Yes
● No

> When you left government, were you able to easily articulate what your value proposition would be to a prospective employer?

ADDITIONAL TRANSITION ASSISTANCE

POLL QUESTION

What additional assistance would have been helpful to you in understanding and articulating your own Value Proposition to a prospective employer?

Most respondents felt they could have used individual coaching and/or clear instruction on developing a value proposition as part of their exit/transition process. Assistance in translating government skills into commercial language would also have been valuable. Respondents also emphasized the value of meeting and talking with people outside of government to understand their focus and priorities. Here are some areas where respondents felt they could have used additional transition help:

> Working with a coach. Having one-on-one help to review resumés and job applications.

> I struggled with my value proposition, specifically I had no idea what it was and never even actively considered it as part of my personal brand until several years post-transition. I probably needed someone to explain it, how to develop it, what potential employers are looking for, and a worksheet to help me develop it.

> Talking to people on the outside and understanding business better. Talk to not only to former government employees. Talk to business leaders who have never served in government. Understand what they know or don't know about your government service and how you can be of value.

> Assistance in translating government and military career experiences to the corporate market place.

> Concrete examples from employers of what skills they found most useful when working with ex-CIA people in the past.

PERSONAL BRANDING – WHAT IS IT?

Personal branding is the story people tell about you when you're not in the room. A personal brand exists separately from a company brand. The process of personal branding involves finding your uniqueness, building a reputation on the things you want to be known for, and then allowing yourself to be known for them.

Carve a niche. This is something to work on prior to separating from government service. Become known as an expert in something. The best personal brands are specifically intended to make you memorable within a targeted community. The narrower and more focused your brand is, the easier it is for people to remember who you are. When it comes time to hire a speaker or a new employee, your narrowed-down brand will be what people remember. Keep your message focused on your target pool of potential employers or professional field. This will make it easier to create content around your personal brand and have others define you. If you're deeply skilled in one area, your reputation alone will help you build the brand you want.

Your personal brand should follow you everywhere you go. It is an authentic representation of who you are and should amplify what you believe. Your personal brand is not only a reflection of a series of job functions like geospatial analyst or IT specialist or Operations Officer, but it also includes your ideals like giving back, thoughtful leadership, or mentorship. All you have in your life is your name and the reputation you garner.

Let other people tell your story. The best public relations for you in your job search is word of mouth via your network. Make your personal brand clear to your friends and contacts so they understand what you want to be known for. Then they can spread the word and help create the buzz around hiring you.

Legacy. Once you've built your personal brand with a reputation and community behind it, the next step is to think about the legacy that you'll leave behind. What are the key words and actions that you want to be known for? Creating the right personal brand will help you be known in your field and consistently land work. It could make the difference in your career between people wondering who you are and people thanking you for your expertise.

. . .

Storytelling. Your ability to "sell yourself" to a prospective employer will also be enhanced by learning effective storytelling. In developing your own "pitch" or "elevator speech" to tell others about what you'd like to do next, consider starting with "why". "Why" is a belief statement. It explains why you do what you do. "Why" can be followed by "what" and "how", but the "why" is what matters most in connecting you to your prospective employer. A good book on this topic is: *Start with "Why"*, by Simon Sinek. (He also does a great Ted Talk on this same topic. *www.ted.-com/talks/simon_sinek_how_great_leaders_inspire_action*)

PERSONAL BRANDING

POLL QUESTION

Do you have advice about developing an appropriate "personal brand" for people coming out of your career field to make them most attractive to future employers? What would that advice be?

One of the most helpful pieces advice from the Interview Subjects was the suggestion that you ask your own colleagues what they think your personal brand would be. What are you known for? What do friends and colleagues believe you most passionate about? Here are their comments:

> Get others who know you to articulate to you what they see as the value and skills you bring. Then do some personal reflection on that. It is not just about personal branding for a job; it is also about your own identity post-retirement. Who are you now? Answer in a way where you don't lose who you were in the Federal Government, but build on it.

" Frankly, your personal brand should have been developed over the arc of your Military / Government career; the last year or two before transition is not the time to do it.

" Know your strengths and your passions.

" Highly recommend articulating what you bring and what you are passionate about.

" Think of your 'personal brand' as the subject heading for your resumé and your elevator pitch. Short, pithy title which conveys what you have to offer.

" Your brand is your passion.

POLL QUESTION

How would you describe your own "personal brand"?

" Able to develop a plan to address any challenge in any culture and to be able to execute it successfully.

" A retired senior CIA paramilitary officer with experience in intelligence and military special operations.

" An investigations leader and problem solver.

" Innovative Global Risk and Cyber Executive.

" Willing to learn, excited to learn, take on new adventures and be gritty about providing value to the company I work for.

" I can teach anybody anything because I love what I do. I'm strategic and I understand organizations. My experience working with partners at a strategic level is a special skill.

" Honest, open communications, trust upfront, willingness to learn, put in the hard work and follow through, follow through, follow though; be responsive and eager.

" I am known as someone who can explain and translate the experience of working in the national security space. I speak to groups about Russian espionage and disinformation.

" Highly accomplished Board member and executive with a mission focus on protecting U.S. economic and national security.

" Thought leader, technically adept, connector, trusted advisor, mentor, coach, adaptable, approachable, giving, caring, passionate, dedicated.

10

APPLICATIONS, THE RESUMÉ, AND COVER LETTERS

The resumé and/or job application MUST be tailored to the specific job you are applying for. *This is very important!*

Many of you in the classified community create an exhaustive Curriculum Vitae to get broad language cleared by a Publications Review Board for future use. This is a good idea; however, you must then pare it down and pull only the most relevant elements of your cleared language into a specific resumé, cover letter, or job application for each job that you apply for. Do not include skills and experiences that are not relevant to the exact position you are applying for. Tailoring the resumé is essential because industry has moved to a machine-readable application process as part of their Applicant Tracking System. This is Artificial Intelligence at work.

Hard but True Fact

When applying to jobs online, no human will ever see your resumé or application unless it precisely mirrors the key wording in the job posting.

To reiterate, your written documentation, which lists your "hard skills" and your "soft skills," needs to use the same language as the employer lists in the job posting (also referred to as a requisition or "req") to ensure that employer's recruiters will actually see your paperwork and evaluate you as a potential match for them. Unless your resumé complies with Artificial Intelligence criteria set out for the specific job, your candidacy likely will not be reviewed by a human (recruiter and/or hiring manager). Failure to tailor a resumé and cover letter to a specific job posting means that many, fairly well-qualified individuals may not even be considered for a job.

Your resumé and/or application should also include a clear Value Statement. Your goal is to be able to say in four to five sentences why someone should hire you over another equally qualified candidate. This is what discriminates you from other applicants and what gets you the job (or not). See the previous chapters on Personal Branding and Value Propositions.

Our government community differs in some ways from the rest of the job-seeking public. Resumés and blind applications for positions advertised on the internet are much less important (and much less successful) than leveraging your personal and professional network to find relevant job opportunities.

According to your colleagues who left government before you, it's not worth a big investment to hire someone to prepare your resumé if you are a retiring government employee. You *will* need a resumé if you are being considered for a position—even a position that you identified through networking, because your contacts will still need to justify to their leadership that you are qualified. However, the expense of hiring a professional resumé writer was not generally recommended by the Interview Subjects.

RESUMÉS AND COVER LETTERS

POLL QUESTION

Did you hire a professional resumé writer? If so, how much did you pay for that service, and were you happy with the result?

> Yep, hired one. I paid around $300–$500 as I recall. The result was fine. However, I found that once I understood the nuance and use of language, formatting, style tips, and what was prioritized and what wasn't in the final result, I could turn out a better product on my own. My advice... save the money and ask a previously successful colleague who has a similar background and career path as yours for their resumé. Use that as a model and guide and develop your own. I was much happier and more successful with my own.

> I paid $1000 for training and a professional resumé service aimed at obtaining "federal employment." The training was good but the resumé didn't prove helpful in getting the job I ultimately accepted. That organization wanted a much shorter resumé than the one the service prepared. I found the service through the Military's transition training program.

> There is no reason whatsoever to do this. The resumé is a piece of paper which satisfies an archaic requirement of traditional stilted HR departments. The resumé as we know it, for people other than entry-level and possibly up to early mid-career people, is obsolete.

POLL QUESTION

If you wrote your own resumés, can you recommend a particular book or set of templates that worked best for you?

Interview Subjects felt that the best templates for writing resumés came from colleagues who had already transitioned. Some also found templates online or through their agency's career transition program materials. Here are some of their comments:

> Found online templates. It would have been good to have a standard set of templates that were visually pleasing. My resumés were rather vanilla looking.

> I used resumés from colleagues who had already left and modified them to fit me. I did like *60 Seconds and You're Hired!* by Robin Ryan for some of the advice.

> I asked for resumés and bios from everyone I knew, looked up resumés on LinkedIn for people in my professions, looked at job postings for companies who hired people for what I wanted to do, and looked up resumé resources on line. I muddled through. But, the ironic thing, my resumé was really just a prop; it was my relationships that opened up doors for me.

> I followed the template provided in the Career Transition Course.

> Trial and error; seek input from outside network; be willing to change resumé.

POLL QUESTION

What resumé-writing tips would you like to share, based upon your transition experience?

Interview Subjects were asked what resumé-writing tips they would like to share with readers. Trends in those responses focused mainly around eliminating acronyms and Federal Government jargon, adding metrics on numbers of people supervised and budgets managed, and paring-down the resumé to 1–2 pages maximum (1 page preferred). Here are some of their tips:

" Put your clearance up front. Don't use acronyms. Don't overdo statistics. Keep it short (2 –3 pages max, with a 1-page version for some situations).

" Be sure to include the number of people you supervised (or the number of embassies you supervised) and the budgets you managed in each of your senior jobs. Avoid acronyms!

" Keep the resumé to a maximum of two pages. Period!

" I wrote a government resumé, not a corporate resumé. The best advice I got was that I needed to translate my government speak into corporate speak. That took a lot of revising with the help of people who hired at the corporate level.

" Adapt your resumé to the specific position.

" If coming from a classified environment that requires review/redaction process, put as much information you can into the resumé. If you provide minimal information, the redaction process may reduce the information available to enable flexibility to adjust your resumé. Having robust information to pull from helps with flexibility to modify your resumé and address the needs of each potential employer.

 Make sure the resumé is translated to language used in the private sector.

AGE-PROOFING A RESUMÉ

The fact is, if your government separation is a retirement, you may be competing with younger people in your pursuit of onward employment. If you are concerned that being a government retiree could subject you to age discrimination, consider ways that you might age-proof your resumé. One way is to avoid saying that you retired from an organization. Another is to learn about what skills are in highest demand now, and seek an additional, marketable qualification while you are still working. For tips on age-proofing your documentation, following helpful article appeared in AARP magazine on "How to Age-Proof your Resumé" (*www.aarp.org/work/job-search/info-2019/age-proof-resume-tips.html*)

11

PROFESSIONAL NETWORKING AND YOUR LINKEDIN PROFILE

If you wish to have paid employment following your Federal Government separation, your most important takeaway from this book should be the *need to leverage your network.* While exact numbers differ, it's safe to say that 70-85% of all jobs are filled through personal and professional networking. Networking is not really about trying to meet as many people as possible. Rather, it is about meeting a few well-connected people who can attest to your abilities and who are willing to refer you to a few other people who are also well-connected.

> *"Over 80% of job seekers say that their network has helped them find work. Networking contacts can help with more than job leads. They can provide referrals or insider information about companies you might be interested in working for. Your network can give you advice on where to look for jobs or review your resumé."*

> — SOURCE: *WWW.THEBALANCECAREERS.COM*

"...85% of critical jobs are filled via networking of some sort, so being highly networked is essential for both the job seekers and for those seeking them. It starts by recognizing no one is average, using the backdoor to find jobs in the hidden market and being different. It ends with hiring better people and getting better jobs."

— SOURCE: *WWW.LINKEDIN.COM/PULSE/NEW-SURVEY-REVEALS-85-ALL-JOBS-FILLED-VIA-NETWORKING-LOU-ADLER/*

Based upon responses to this survey, the benefits of tapping your professional and personal network to find a new opportunity are even higher for Federal Government employees transitioning out than for the general population, due to the unique nature of our experiences.

You have worked with amazing people from across your professional community over the course of your career. Your network is not just from your own specific agency or job field—but by virtue of your long tenure and our integrated community—you have established many contacts from across government agencies. Just getting the word out that you are preparing to leave government is a great start. Tell your work colleagues. (Some are reluctant to do this out of fear of being considered a "lame duck" at work, but this is short-sighted.) Tell your neighbors. Tell your spouse's friends. The best place to start is with your former colleagues who retired before you. You may have lost touch with some of them. Find a way to reach out to get reacquainted. Do a little online research, and you can locate just about anyone. You will be pleasantly surprised how helpful former colleagues will be.

A good place to start the conversation is to ask them about their own career transition and any advice/guidance they might have. You might also ask them to review your resumé and make comments on how to make it stronger. These contacts may not know of a specific opportunity for you to pursue right now, but they will certainly keep you in mind when they talk with their other friends and hear about potential positions that might be a good fit for you. A key part of effective networking is being clear about your employment goals. A careful self-assessment can provide clear information about who you are and what you want when communicating with contacts. Prepare talking points and practice delivering them, whether you have 10 seconds for an elevator pitch, 60 seconds for a commercial, or 30 minutes for an information-seeking interview. My favorite approach is to invite someone for coffee and ask them about their own transition.

MAPPING A NETWORK FOR JOB HUNTING

Your network will include people you know well, acquaintances and referrals. It can also include people you had brief contact within the course of your career. Be creative. Here's a partial list of common sources for networking contacts:

- Work training classmates
- Contacts from Embassy postings or Joint Center assignments
- Former work colleagues, including from other agencies and related career fields
- School classmates (any grade or school)
- Community clubs
- Former employers, including supervisors and co-workers
- Friends and relatives, local and out-of-town
- Hobby groups, such as bridge clubs, gardening, model trains, or quilting
- Members of clubs, such as a running group, tennis team, health club, softball team, or hiking club
- Members of your church, temple, synagogue or mosque (some religious organizations also sponsor job search groups)
- Military friends
- Neighbors, current and former

- Participants in trade shows, seminars, or workshops you've attended
- Political groups
- Professional associations (see the list provided by our Interview Subjects)
- Local professionals you deal with, such as attorneys, accountants, doctors, dentists, insurance agents, pharmacists, and veterinarians
- Service or fraternal organizations and groups
- Services, such as travel agents, stockbrokers, or realtors
- Volunteer associations, past and present

Keep track of your contacts. Collect business cards and then either manually enter them into a list or scan them into a contact management tool. When a contact provides you with leads or referrals, be sure to ask for their permission to use their name. Keep detailed records of your networking activity. To whom did you speak, about what, when, and what were the results? For each contact, identify next steps and develop a reliable follow-up system. Try a spreadsheet, although a collection of index cards will also work. At the very least, consider a notebook or computer application. The key is to be persistent and be sure to follow-up quickly on any leads that are provided to you.

Thank everyone who helps you (in person, by email, or with a letter to follow-up). Keep those who are interested posted on the progress of your job search or career change. Remember also to make yourself available as a resource for other jobseekers and treat them as you would like to be treated by those with whom you network.

Keep your professional network alive. Join your organization's Retiree Association if they have one (e.g., CIA Retirees Association). Talk with people who have transitioned in many different directions and ask their perspective on the path they took.

PROFESSIONAL NETWORKING

POLL QUESTION

What industry-specific professional associations have been helpful to you in expanding your professional network? How have you used them to your advantage?

Here are the various organizations that the Interview Subjects found helpful for networking during their professional transition.

- CIA Retirees Association (CIRA)
- CIA Officers Memorial Foundation
- Washington Executive (Washington Exec)
- Intelligence and National Security Alliance (INSA)
- International Spy Museum
- American Academy of Diplomacy
- American Society for Industrial Security (ASIS)
- Society of Former Special Agents
- Office of Strategic Services (OSS) Society
- Wounded Warriors
- Center for Strategic and International Studies
- Foreign Policy Institute
- Armed Forces Communications and Electronics Association (AFCEA)
- Naval Intelligence Professionals (NIP)
- Association for Talent Development
- Association of Former Intelligence Officers (AFIO)
- The Cipher Brief
- The Retired General and Flag officer network (TFGON)
- LinkedIn
- Surface Navy Association
- Foreign Area Officers Association
- International Coach Federation (ICF)

- Society for Human Resource Management (SHRM)
- Cyber Conferences
- Chief Information Security Officer (CISO) organizations
- National Military Intelligence Association (NMIA)
- National Association of Corporate Directors (NACD)
- The U.S. Geospatial Intelligence Foundation (USGIF)

POLL QUESTION

What personal and professional networking tips would you like to share with your government colleagues who are currently considering a career transition?

Interview Subjects' tips most often emphasized the importance of using your existing network, and also broadening that network by joining relevant organizations.

> Have information-seeking coffees and lunches with people, not to ask for a job, but to ask about their experiences and their organization. Call upon our professional community alumni. Everyone in the tribe is incredibly generous with their time and advice.

> When you go to think-tank events and other events at which private sector and Private Voluntary Organization (PVO) or Non-governmental Organization (NGO) colleagues are present, seek them out and tell them of your up-coming retirement and availability.

> Consider joining an association that best suits you. In my case, I became an active member in the Special Forces Association chapter near me as well as becoming a Rotary Club member.

" Network, network, network. Don't be afraid to reach out to that person that you "kind of knew" to refresh your network —they may be your best help. It's like fishing—the more lines you have in the water, the more likely you will get a bite.

" Make a list of everyone you know and start with them— send notes, invite them to lunch, coffee, or dinner, or for a phone call; be genuinely interested in them and prepare for your discussions with them; ask them for how they can help you and if there is anything you can do for them; follow up with a thank you and ask if they would be willing to introduce you to anyone in their network. Reach out, cold call, ask— you will be amazed by the positive response!

NETWORKING THROUGH LINKEDIN

What is LinkedIn? LinkedIn is a social media platform geared toward professional networking for the business world. Individuals, companies, and agencies set up "profiles" containing their basic background, to which they post content of that might be of interest to others. You build a network by connecting with others with whom you find common professional interests or backgrounds. There is a robust search capability on the platform to find other people, jobs, companies, content, schools, and groups that fit your search criteria. LinkedIn also has a private messaging capability that allows you to reach out to privately message someone, whether or not you know them. LinkedIn has deep capabilities and content at no cost. They also offer a subscription to a "Premium" service which provided additional services. (The author has not found significant added value for paid content on LinkedIn Premium, but others have found value in using it.)

LinkedIn is *not* Facebook for adults. It is not the forum for jokes, cartoons, or social commentary. It is considered inappropriate to post anything political (although some people do). LinkedIn is for sharing and exchanging business-related content.

While LinkedIn can be considered taboo in intelligence circles, and it feels very uncomfortable for people who have been working under cover or in a classified environment, it is a legitimate tool in the business world. Almost all prospective employers consider it an important tool to convey industry trends, to dialogue on advances in their industry, to announce contract wins, to find new talent—and importantly—to verify the legitimacy of job applicants. It is also a very important professional networking tool in industry. Therefore, as awkward as it feels, having at least a basic LinkedIn profile is quite important if you are seeking employment outside the government. One useful resource on LinkedIn is the book: *"How to Write a Killer LinkedIn Profile... and 18 Mistakes to Avoid"* by Brenda Bernstein

LinkedIn Learning. Another benefit of LinkedIn is LinkedIn Learning. It contains courses available online for how to set up your LinkedIn profile which will help you optimize it for your purposes. (There are plenty of other articles on the internet with tips on setting up your LinkedIn profile too.) LinkedIn Learning also has training courses in how to create a perfect elevator pitch, personal branding, resumé-writing techniques, interview skills, and developing a career search strategy. It is a powerful resource.

Survey respondents generally saw high value in setting up a LinkedIn profile and using the tool as a resource to research companies and people. Some found job leads that way. Others used it to network and market themselves. Respondents found value to following industry trends and thought leadership on LinkedIn. Several respondents were uncomfortable with the tool because of counterintelligence concerns. Here are some of their thoughts on using LinkedIn, tips on setting up your profile, discussion on how often they use LinkedIn, comments about the value of using

LinkedIn messaging as an outreach tool, and the range of functions they use most.

POLL QUESTION

What are your thoughts on using LinkedIn as a job search resource? If you use LinkedIn, do you have tips to share for setting up an effective online profile on LinkedIn?

Nearly all survey respondents to this question were positive about the use of LinkedIn as a tool for research, networking and job search. Several mentioned being wary of putting too much information online because of counter-intelligence concerns. Here are some of their comments:

> LinkedIn was a rich resource for me. I used it less for job search than preparing for transition, resumé writing, professional networking. I still value it three years later.

> I found it useful as a networking tool and from there working to get jobs. I did get interviews from job postings I applied to and I recently hired someone from a cold application to a LinkedIn job posting I put up.

> It is a great resource! I used it extensively—to figure out what skills and certifications people had in my profession, who they worked for, and who they were connected to. It was invaluable.

> Do *not* use your government portrait with a flag on it as your LinkedIn profile picture. This is bad form because you no longer represent the Federal Government. Industry has different rules. Have a new headshot taken for LinkedIn, either formal or informal, depending upon the image that

you wish to convey to prospective employers and your network.

Good to understand what is potentially out there and compare and contrast. Also good as a tool to build a personal brand or garner potential attention or interest in you and your profile through posting and updates to your activities. Decent as a communication tool with contacts and network. Bad as a way to identify, apply for, and pursue a particular job.

I am wary of LinkedIn due to its potential use by foreign governments or bad actors. I have considered shutting down my account but am unwilling to take that step yet. I ignore offers I get unless I know the person reaching out.

I have gotten great leads on opportunities through LinkedIn.

I think LinkedIn is necessary. It is what every employer or contact will look at before meeting you. Most employers expect that people have information available on-line.

Great resource. When eligible, obtain a LinkedIn account and keep in touch with former colleagues and work professionals. It's all about networking.

Personally, I didn't like it. It was akin to a blind date. I didn't feel comfortable putting previous employment information out there. Nor was I comfortable with a stranger reaching out to me to discuss my experiences. I prefer the personal approach.

> LinkedIn is has emerged as an almost indispensable professional resource. I could not be effective as an independent advisor/consultant without it. I use it every day.

POLL QUESTION

If you use LinkedIn, what tips would you share for setting up an effective online profile on LinkedIn?

> It can be uncomfortable putting yourself out there as Intel after having been under wraps for so long. Think hard about what you put online because it is there forever. Look at others' profiles first to determine what you might be comfortable with. Go slow.

> Post things on your LinkedIn page. It gets you "views" and you need views. Also, put up a decent picture—not too formal, but not too casual either. I had the traditional head shot with the U.S. flag in the background, but it didn't make me look approachable, and it didn't make me stand out. If you have no picture, I likely won't accept a connection from you. And your resumé on LinkedIn matters. There are classes you can take on this topic and some of them are pretty useful; however, some of them want you to pay a bunch of money for the privilege—ignore those.

> Start (on LinkedIn) early in the transition process because it takes time. Being able to communicate with former colleagues/associates you would not otherwise chat with is extremely valuable. Let people know you are looking for a job.

Put your whole name and a picture in addition to a good profile of who you are. Be selective with whom you link. My LinkedIn network fits pretty neatly into my interests—not just any person who asks.

Be very clear on your Value Proposition and play to that. It's an online job search board, so think through your key words.

Take it seriously. Take the time to present yourself in a way that will appeal to potential contacts and employees. Use pictures and materials. Make it a place where someone can get a feel for you. It is more important than a resumé.

Be careful as these are seen and monitored by other intel services across the globe. I would not recommend including a resumé on LinkedIn (but that's just me). You can always send your cleared resumé to a company via email and not post those details on line.

POLL QUESTION

Have you used LinkedIn messaging to reach out to strangers who work in areas that interest you? Was that ever productive?

I like doing this. Most people are helpful and responsive.

Yes, I used it to reach out to a retired agent who ran a networking site, and he spent an hour with me on the phone walking me through career transition topics. It was the best hour I spent during my job search.

" I have had some success with LinkedIn messaging—which resulted in a great phone call with a fellow college alum about his business, an in-person meeting (in another city), and eventual job offer with an entrepreneur who started her own and now very successful coaching company, several offers to connect me with others who may be more helpful to my search (with two of the three following through), and people reaching out to me who did not have my email address but saw my profile and wanted to connect, which resulted in new business.

" Absolutely. I've gained consulting/advising clients and valuable connections via LinkedIn Messaging. With a paid premium account, you can reach out to anyone. It is a very powerful and potentially very valuable tool.

POLL QUESTION

How often do you use LinkedIn now and for what purposes?

" I use it daily to read articles and see what people in my network are doing. I also use it to help identify potential positions for my clients as a coach.

" I use it all the time to maintain my network, and you never know when a better opportunity will present itself. Plus, the one thing people need to realize about the private sector is that the winds could change tomorrow, and you could be out of a job. Better have a Plan B.

" I use LinkedIn several times a week and mostly for research and to follow people.

I use it every day to keep connected with people and to market myself and my company.

I was on LinkedIn every week when I was transitioning and job hunting. Three years later, I use it to keep up with work friends and see what others are doing. People still check me out and contact me with job offers.

I use it often and to educate myself on the industry.

POLL QUESTION

Are there other online networking resources that you would recommend for jobseekers?

Interview Subjects recommended the following additional online (and other) networking resources in addition to the organizations previously mentioned and LinkedIn:

 *Indeed.com*

 *Glassdoor.com*

I attended some Military base transition training, which was sponsored and taught by local recruiters in the DC area, and that was an invaluable resource and connection.

" Find people who are connectors—I have a couple in (a major city near where I live), and I'm very generous with my network to those that want access.

" Don't ignore your Facebook and Twitter presence! Each can attract or repel prospective employers. Your social media profile is important these days.

" I use Twitter as a platform to demonstrate thought leadership. Upon leaving the government, I started a Facebook account but deleted it less than 24 hours as I found it creepy and intrusive. I did keep investing time (and money) into LinkedIn and Twitter, and it has paid off significantly.

12

INTERVIEWING STRATEGIES

Now that you have determined your specific technical skills and your soft skills; assessed your values and your motivators; determined your "personal brand"; drafted a resumé and set-up a LinkedIn profile; it is time to think about how you can best present yourself in an interview.

You will find that, for the most part, your private sector counterparts will convey a deep respect for you and what you did for the government. They will generally avoid asking details and specifics because they want to avoid making you feel awkward (and also wish to avoid knowing more than they should). Don't interpret this lack of questioning as disinterest in you or your background. They are simply trying to respect you and the information you had access to.

Employers are increasingly using a variety of tools and approaches to connect with and assess potential candidates, not only against a role's requirements, but also cultural fit. The use of videoconferencing; online testing, and assessments, and a search of your social media presence is now commonplace. You need to be able to demonstrate that you have reviewed the company's website; have a good understanding of the company's market, competitors, product/solution, and service offerings, and their communicated market differentiators.

Video-conference screening, online testing, and technical interviews have become more and more common, particularly after the Covid-19 pandemic, which precluded in-person interviews for an extended period of time. You need to treat these interviews the same as a face-to-face interview (i.e,. be available at the designated time; ensure in advance that you can connect to the video-conference link; make sure you are in a location that is quiet and private with limited distractions; dress appropriately, and be ready with questions around the company, the specific role, the working environment, to include having a copy of the job description or job posting handy).

Finally, it should be noted that employers are increasingly looking for cultural fit with their organizations and core values as part of the recruitment and selection process. You need to understand the company's mission, vision, values, and be able to address questions around working environment, management style and emotional intelligence with ease, consistent with the level of the position against which you have applied.

INTERVIEW TIPS

√ **If you are leaving the Federal Government**, telling a prospective employer that you "can't talk about it," or "it's classified," and being coy about your National Security career will not win you a job. In fact, it is very off-putting. Finding the right language to describe your concrete skill sets and your value add (without exposing sources and methods) is very important. For those involved in conducting either Diplomacy or Human Intelligence, for example, this might include skills like:

- Building strong customer relationships
- Conducting needs assessments
- Detail-orientation
- Business development
- Strategic and tactical planning
- Ensuring compliance with regulations

- Cross-cultural sensitivity

Review the marketable skills chapter for additional language.

√ **Avoid acronyms in the interview process**. Don't use any at all. TDY, PCS, any organizational abbreviations or jargon will only confuse the interviewer. Wikipedia has a Military acronym translator that you may find helpful: *https://en.wikipedia.org/wiki/Glossary_of_military_abbreviations*.

√ **Go High.** Avoid speaking negatively of anyone, any organization, or any company in your interviews. Many people are leaving their Federal Government careers at a time when they may have had a professional setback, had ethical concerns, or possibly hit a glass ceiling. These are normal transition points. Take the lessons learned and look forward. The job interview is the time to focus on all the positive experiences you have had and the skills that you bring, because nobody wants to hire someone who is toxic, won't accept responsibility, places blame on others, or otherwise can't get out of a negative loop.

√ **Be Prepared to Talk about Your Weaknesses and Failures.** Do so in ways that take responsibility and do not put blame on anyone else.

√ **Be Prepared and Familiar with the Organization's Website and Leadership.** Know their business line and their capabilities/products. Research their financials if you can. Review their press releases.

√ **Review the Job Description.** Make notes about how your qualifications specifically fit the job description, so you can speak to why you're a strong candidate for the position.

√ **Have a Friend or Family Member Conduct a Mock Interview.** Record it so you can hear how you sound. Once you have a recording, you'll be able to hear your "ums," "uhs," and "okays," so you can practice reducing them from your conversational speech. Listening to the recording will also help you pinpoint answers that you can improve.

In addition to the insights from our Interview Subjects in this book, be sure to talk with others who have already successfully transitioned about their interview experiences.

A great source for job search and interviewing tips is the website: *www.thebalancecareers.com*

INTERVIEWING

POLL QUESTION

How many different companies did you interview with before landing the first job out of government?

Interviewing experiences were varied with our Interview Subjects. Common practice seemed to be to consider a range of business areas, do some interviews for practice, and to explore potential paths, and then narrow down your interests from the feedback and feelings you had. Interviewees explored up to 18 different organizations before settling on what they eventually wanted to do.

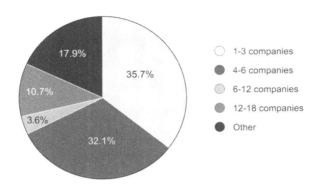

How many different companies/ organizations did you interview with before landing your first job out of government?

POLL QUESTION

How many interviews did you have for the position that you ultimately took? What types of interviews were they?

Interview Subjects had from one to six interviews for the one position to which they were ultimately hired. Interview types included: headhunter/recruiter interviews, phone interviews, 1:1 interviews, HR interviews, team/panel interviews, formal and informal interviews, interviews with Hiring Managers, meetings with the CEO and senior executives, down to the most junior employee.

POLL QUESTION

Did you practice for your interviews? Did you do this alone or by using mock interviews?

Survey respondents discussed their preparation for interviews. Practicing likely questions and answers was an important part of their preparation, along with reviewing their resumé against the requirements for the position and doing extensive research on the company and its leadership.

> Talk with others about the interviews they had there. Glassdoor is very helpful for insights on questions, employee reviews of management, and common salaries.

> I educated myself on the company and on the individual that was going to be interviewing me. LinkedIn is a wealth of information on individuals, and I like *Finding Alpha* by Eric Falkenstein for information on publicly traded companies. I went through my resumé and looked for areas that they might have questions. I went through the job posting and came up with areas I thought I could add value and came up with short descriptions of how to communicate that. I also prepared examples of things that I had done that matched the job posting requirements.

> Lots of prep and practice: I made a list of all the key points that I wanted them to know about me, no matter what they asked; made a list of possible questions to include behavioral questions I would be asked and practiced my responses, with examples; researched the company, its leadership, values, employees, online reviews and awards, and offerings, so I could talk about alignment, how I would see myself fitting in and contributing, and have good questions to ask them (what inspires and motivates them about the company and working there, how they would describe the company's impact and value added; and talked with people who had worked with or for the company.

" Consulted the website. consulted with friends/colleagues who were clients or on the board of the company; received recommendations from these people.

" Tailored it to the job description. Highlighted my talents and personality that fit the task and the client. Tried not to be distracted by the company's razzmatazz. Knew my $ bottom line and how much I was willing to negotiate, and did not focus on $ until the end.

" Did research on the company. Identified priorities and core values. Also looked at goals and projections for the coming year. Decided how I could talk about how I reflected those values in my own experience and how I could specifically help achieve organizational priorities. If I could determine specific individuals I'd be talking to, I did a bit of research on them...background, hobbies, items of commonality, etc. to be prepared to build rapport. Reviewed my own skills and came prepared with vignettes to highlight how those came into play. Prepared also to discuss typical strengths, weaknesses, desires, goals, and why I wanted to work for this company, and why I'd be a good fit for them. Also prepared a list of questions for them that reflected insight and reflective thought about the position.

" Did a mock murder board and reviewed literature on interview questions and techniques I read and worked through the book *Acing the Interview* by Tony Beshara. It provided excellent insights into the interview process, who participates, what each of them wants, and the phases of an interview. The book then provides sample questions directed at those phases of the interviews and tips on how to construct answers.

Anticipate likely questions and prepare the answers. Also be prepared to go with the flow, as the interviewer may have a different script!

I discussed the company with the friend who was trying to recruit me—what he liked/didn't like, mission, customers etc.

I had written notes and worked hard to demonstrate I had done research (web, discussions, etc.) to learn about their company, my prospective role, and my vision for how I would contribute to the company's progress.

POLL QUESTION

What tips would you like to share for successful personal interviews, based upon your transition experience?

Interview Subjects provided valuable tips for readers who are preparing for interviews. These tips are focused on two main areas: appropriate demeanor for the interview, and the need to have done adequate research and preparation. Here are some of their highlights:

Be concise. Have stories to tell to illustrate your value proposition. Research your interviewer and find things in common with them. Research the company, their website, their mission, and their financials. Show that you cared enough to do your homework.

Be sure to sound interested in the organization and have a couple of good questions to ask to demonstrate that interest.

There's going to be a question you hope they won't ask—have a good answer for it. Also, be complete in your answers to questions, but be organized and not too long. Nobody wants to hire the person who gives you twenty minutes on "tell me a little about yourself." If you've spoken for more than two minutes in an answer, it's probably too long. Be prepared to give two-minute-or-less answers to common questions. And I'm looking for fit—if you're not a good fit, neither one of us is going to be happy, so be yourself. Also, recognize that when I interview you, it's not like in the government. If you don't work out, that could cost me my job, so recognize and appreciate that I'm taking a risk. Convince me that risk is worth my while.

Be genuine. Express an eagerness to learn and do whatever it takes to help the company succeed. Be honest about the areas that you are unfamiliar with but express interest/eagerness to learn and take on these challenges. When CEO asked "Do you want to do business development or business operations?," the answer is whatever you need the most, unless there is a compelling reason not to say that.

Show enthusiasm, lessons learned, flexibility, ability, desire to continue learning, humility, openness, respectfulness. If you describe your professional skills with a genuine love of service and personal authenticity instead of arrogance, it gives off an undeniable confidence. Have in your head the type of person you are competing against, and show how you are different/better. Be open in your demeanor, but not overly effusive. Listen carefully to what the interviewer is asking. Think about the question/statement before responding. Be very aware of your own body language and the interviewers to assess possible changes in direction.

Be honest and true to yourself. Don't oversell or understate yourself. If the company is not interested, then it was not meant to be—there will be other opportunities. Regardless of former positions held, be humble and respectful.

Military and government leaders are raised to be self-effacing, contrite, and to deflect credit to others. Interviewing is the time to appropriately tell your story and take due credit for your accomplishments (without embellishment).

13

UNDERSTANDING CORPORATE BENEFIT OPTIONS AND NEGOTIATING YOUR CONTRACT

Of our Interview Subjects, 73% listed compensation as one of their top priorities in deciding what to do after separation. Most of those chose to pursue some sort of full-time corporate role. On top of compensation, 23% of our Interview Subjects expressed interest in specific benefits, such as 401k, insurance and PTO. The benefits that you carry from your government career into your post-retirement or post-separation work will vary and depend upon the agency from which you are leaving. For most of us, the world of corporate compensation and benefits is foreign.

As you evaluate your future opportunities, it is important to understand a prospective employer's group and voluntary benefits program as part of the decision-making process around a given role/opportunity and employment offer (i.e., be an educated consumer). Applicants will want to consider an employment offer based upon their understanding of the role, their expected contribution, the working environment, and base and incentive compensation terms, Employer and voluntary benefits, however, are also an important part of the overall compensation package. When you are discussing a potential job offer, listen carefully to the full package offered and not just the base salary.

. . .

Most employers offer a range of standard benefits that employees expect to receive as part of a total compensation package. These include medical, dental, vision, group term life, short and long-term disability, and a retirement savings plan. Generally speaking, after base compensation, the most important benefits are medical coverage and a retirement savings plan, to include an employer contribution or match given the cost of contributory medical premiums, and the ability to supplement retirement income through an employer tax-deferred or Roth savings plan, with an employer-vested contribution/match. Those entering the job market with existing medical coverage as part of their current retirement terms need to pay particular attention to medical coverage continuation options (COBRA) and costs with a prospective employer, as these are limited and can be costly. *Premium costs for employer-provided medical cover are material and may provide an opportunity for you to negotiate additional base compensation, or additional benefits such as paid leave, where your existing Federal Government medical coverage can be continued through retirement.* Also, if you are a government retiree, your benefits needs may differ from the standard jobseeker. This could play to your advantage, because a prospective employer may not need to pay for your health insurance, making you more financially attractive as an applicant.

Here are some examples of benefits that could become part of an offer package in the private sector:

The Value of a Clearance. No company has the ability to sponsor an individual for a new security clearance. If a position is advertised as requiring a clearance, it means that the company will only hire someone who comes with a valid, current clearance. Their government customer must sponsor and pay for any new clearance. The cost of a top-secret security clearance is $10,000 to $15,000 per individual. As a result, companies are eagerly seeking to employ individuals who already have the needed clearances. *This could translate into additional money for you if you already have clearances. Some companies have been known to pay individuals the equivalent of the cost of a clearance as a one-time sign-on bonus for joining with a clearance.*

Health Insurance. A number of health insurance products are on the open market, with many employers offering a range of insurance options to meet varying employee demographics, cover needs for themselves and eligible dependents, while keeping overall premium and employee contribution costs affordable. For smaller employers, the range of options can often be more limited as they have less negotiating power with the insurance companies, and a limited budget to cover premium costs. In general, employers look to provide a fully insured medical insurance plan to their employees through either a preferred provider organization (PPO) and/or a health maintenance organization (HMO). A PPO has the advantage of allowing covered employees and their eligible dependents more flexibility to see a physician within or out of network (subject to plan limits), while an HMO requires that all care be managed through a dedicated health management organization. With escalating healthcare costs, employers are also looking at increasing self-insured insurance plans and high-deductible plans (with either a Health Savings Account or Health Reimbursement Account) as a means to provide employees with cover options, while keeping escalating costs under control. The health insurance environment through employer-provided plans now expects employees to be more educated about (and take more responsibility for) the choice and management of their health care option choices and the management of their healthcare costs at the point of service.

If you are a Federal Government retiree entering the job market with existing health insurance in place, you are at a distinct advantage, and need to be careful to weigh existing cover and costs with a new employer's plan. Of particular importance is the ability and cost to continue medical coverage post-employment with a new employer, as continuation through COBRA is expensive (i.e,. the full premium cost as the employer premium contribution ceases plus an administration fee is charged by a third-party COBRA administrator). COBRA is for a defined and limited period of time under COBRA provisions.

Finally, if you waive coverage with a new position you may also be able to negotiate additional base compensation or benefits (e.g., sign-on bonus or additional paid leave) Please note, though, that not all employers will provide additional base compensation or benefits, if they wish to maintain consistency between employees at the same level.

Dental Insurance. Dental insurance is a standard employer-provided benefit that is generally inexpensive for an employer to provide, unless orthodontic benefits are provided to adults. Most dental insurance provides for employees and their covered dependents to receive up to two cleanings/check-ups within a 12-month period (generally separated by six months) with no copayment or deductible, with additional services being subject to a deductible and a co-pay up to an annual benefit reimbursement maximum of $1,000–$1,500, depending on plan limits. Dental plans generally provide both in-network and out-of-network benefits, but out-of-network benefits are generally less and are subject to reasonable and customary rules by the insurer. Therefore, it is more cost-effective to use an in-network provider as much as possible.

401k—Retirement Savings Plan. The continued ability to contribute towards retirement savings and to receive an employer tax-deferred contribution into a retirement savings account is a wise tax-deferral strategy against employment income. The IRS sets an annual dollar limit each tax year on the amount that an employee can contribute into a retirement savings plan, with an additional catch-up contribution currently allowed for plan participants aged 50 or above in the plan year. Employers, through their plan providers, allow participants to set their own contribution amounts either as percentage or flat dollar amounts against plan-eligible income. This may allow contributions to be made on a tax-deferred or non-tax deferred basis (Roth), and will generally provide for an employer contribution or match to an employee's account on a tax-deferred basis.

For the employer's contribution to a savings plan, it is important to know:

1. When the employer actually makes their match contribution (with each payroll cycle, quarterly, or following the end of the plan year);
2. When the employer contribution is considered vested (actually in the participant's hands). This vesting can be: *A.* immediately, *B.* after a certain length of service (cliff vesting), or *C.* over a period of service on a pro-rated basis.

Questions around vesting are worth asking, because a prospective employer may try to entice you with a high employer match but could require you to work for several years before you are actually eligible to receive their vested match. This can potentially lock you in to an employment situation for years because you don't want to lose the matching funds.

Also, it is important to ask questions around a 401k plan's ability and terms around participant loans, in-service, and hardship withdrawals. While it is generally not considered wise to withdraw from a 401k plan short of retirement eligibility, you should be clear on provisions for a participant's access to his/her account balance, terms of any loan provisions, and restrictions and excise taxes that may apply for any withdrawals allowed. As a retiree, advice and guidance from your financial planner is strongly advised, but it is generally unwise to leave an employer's tax-deferred contribution to retirement on the table and leave short of the vesting period.

The terms of a company's 401k plan are not negotiable. You either choose to contribute or you don't. You cannot ask for a higher match or a shorter vesting period, for example. This is because an employer purchases a set plan from a vendor which provides uniform benefits for all employees in the company.

√ **TIP**: With the wide range of 401k plans available in 2020, an employer 401k match of 4% is considered average in the Washington, DC area, with 2% considered "low", and a 6+% match considered "generous". The ideal is to be offered a 401k plan that vests immediately. There are employers who offer immediate vesting, although the majority of employers seem to require a vesting period of 2–4 years.

Profit Sharing Plans/Employee Incentive Schemes. Depending on the role and the level of the position offered, variable or incentive compensation may be an important part of an overall compensation package. Incentive compensation can range from:

1. A sign-on bonus which will generally be tied to a continuing service period of 12–24 months;
2. Commission-based plans for business development and revenue/sales generation;
3. An overall corporate bonus/profit sharing plan that provides for an annual bonus based upon overall company performance metrics;
4. Individual performance bonuses;
5. "Just-in-time" employee bonus payments such as Spot Awards that can either be monetary or non-monetary.

These incentive schemes focus on providing additional cash compensation to an eligible participant based upon defined metrics. If such plans are part of an overall compensation package, it is important for you to understand eligibility; plan performance metrics; payment, and vesting to make sure that such plans have a reasonable chance of a payment being made, and that the company has a history of making the required payments.

Work-Life Balance. These benefits often include flexible work schedules, paid time off (e.g. vacation, sick leave, and other paid leave).

Work/life balance, and the ability to have some flexibility in terms of work schedule and location (work from home) are important things to consider as part of your employment experience. Remote work opportunities are on the increase, and many employers support a remote work location for part or all of the work week. This needs to be carefully explored/considered as part of an agreed work schedule, noting though that remote working can work well for some, it can be less than desirable for others as it can lead to a disconnected feeling from an employer and/or work team, and does not meet the need for those seeking social engagement as part of the work-experience.

Paid Time Off (PTO). PTO comes in many forms, including vacation, paid sick leave, and other paid leave, such as educational, jury, and bereavement. Increasingly, employers are combining vacation and sick leave into a single category of Paid Time Off. It is important to understand an employer's policy regarding paid leave (i.e., eligibility, levels based upon years of service, request and approval process, and whether any paid leave balance is paid out or forfeited with separation from employment).

Equity Participation. Outside of cash-based compensation (to include salary, bonus and commission opportunities, and other variable cash-based compensation plans or programs), you will also want to understand an employee's ability to participate in the equity (i.e., ownership), of an employer company. This form of compensation is generally geared towards a longer-term retention strategy for key employees and/or those who contribute to the building of shareholder value. You should understand whether the employer will provide you with an opportunity to buy company shares at a discounted price under a qualified Employee Stock Purchase Plan (ESPP); whether company shares/options form part of a bonus or performance plan, and how performance based are awarded and issued (e.g., shares, stock options, stock appreciation rights, or restricted stock units). Equity participation is beneficial in that it is generally tax deferred as non-cash compensation until a qualifying event occurs, but it is important to understand how such plans work, to include eligibility; awards levels and vehicles; vesting schedule; personal income tax implications for any awards, and the status of any awards and action required upon separation of employment.

Voluntary Benefits. In addition to the standard benefit offerings to employees, an employer may make available a range of voluntary benefits, either at a group discount or without charge. These can include an Employee Assistance Program (EAP); office meals and snacks; access to a gym or a discounted membership to a local gym; parking or a transportation allowance, and access to discounted insurance products while employed (e.g., voluntary life insurance, voluntary disability insurance, or pet insurance).

14

CONCLUSION AND FINAL CAREER ADVICE

I wrote this book to help Intelligence, Foreign Affairs, Military, National Security, and other Federal Government professionals approach the daunting task of leaving their current government service, whether through retirement or resignation. Readers have lauded the guidance and wisdom provided here by more than 30 former government professionals from CIA, NSA, FBI, State Department, NGA, the U.S. Military and Treasury. They have been a tremendous resource.

I hope that you will use this guide, as well as your personal and professional network, to explore the wide range of next step options available to you. When I left the CIA, there was no "handbook" for those considering leaving government service. I wished that there had been one.

In this Guide, we have discussed reasons why people generally decide to separate from the government and also provided some questions to ask yourself in making the decision to leave. We commented on the various human factors to consider in making your transition such as mental and physical health, along with the positives and not-so-positive aspects of making such a big life change. We talked about how to prepare yourself for making a change, such as the importance of financial readiness and evaluating whether or not to pursue a second career. You were presented with a range of some potential next-steps to consider (from jumping straight into full retirement to pursuing full-time employment and various options in-between). The Guide outlined some major steps in the career transition process for Government professionals, such as thinking through your own life goals and developing vision for the future. We provided listings of marketable skills relevant to people coming from the Government sector. The Guide also discussed developing a job search strategy, determining your value proposition, personal branding, drafting resumés, professional networking and the use of LinkedIn. We also provided tips on interviewing, and negotiating an employment agreement if you elect to pursue onward employment.

The book includes practical worksheet exercises to help you evaluate your readiness to leave; your current family budget and resulting salary requirements; your level of ambition; your vision for the future; the legacy you would like to leave behind; your personal and professional goals; your workplace values along with questions to consider when evaluating an offer of employment. These are deep topics, so carve out some dedicated time to think through your priorities.

In conclusion, please consider these final pieces of advice from our Interview Subjects, whose over-riding message to you is that planning for your future is key. *Career transition is an opportunity*. Look back and take pride in your past achievements. Evaluate your strengths, passions, life priorities, and vision for the future. Then move forward to select a next step that plays to your strengths, key motivators and personal/professional values.

FINAL POLL QUESTION

Is there any other advice that you would give to transitioning employees?

66 I always tell folks not to rush leaving their Agency careers— they've worked hard to get to their level, and they should retire on their own terms.

66 Retirement planning actually has to start earlier than the transition point. You must prepare yourself early in your career for retirement. Invest in the Thrift Savings Plan (TSP) as much as you can—every time you get a raise, put it into your TSP. Then when your retirement date comes up, you can do it and never have to look back on it. Then once you retire, do things you enjoy, might never had time for before, and meet new people.

66 Be patient and truly understand what motivates you and your passion, and don't worry about having to change jobs to find the right fit for you.

66 Appropriately celebrate the closure of a great career and be open to new things and new ideas. It is like graduating from high school or college all over again!

66 Don't be afraid. Believe in yourself. Your network is your net worth. You will have to prove yourself early and often on "the outside." You've spent 30 years earning a reputation, and you can lose it in five minutes with a breach of ethics.

66 You are unlikely to replicate the experience you have had in the IC. Enjoy it knowing that there is very interesting and rewarding work beyond the Federal Government.

66 There will be no better time to take risks and pursue what you want to do. Don't have regrets by not pursuing your dreams.

66 Remember, life is short. There are more important things in life than making money. Do you know what those are?

66 Keep calm and carry on!

66 Your next life is what you make it!

66 My experience is that it took several years before I understood where I wanted to go, and what I wanted to do.

66 Be honest with yourself. Prioritize what is important to you. Talk and discuss all aspects with spouse and family. Make a financial plan.

66 Think long and hard about whether you want to start a second career or transition. If you are financially and mentally comfortable to consider a life of being able to make personal decisions free of having to factor in job responsibilities.

66 Take time to breathe.

Be patient. Be honest with your friends. Your honesty will help them. If you are lucky enough to have enough money to retire, do something you love.

Understand what you want before you begin a search; stay true to your objectives; take your time.

Do not leave in a negative mindset regarding your career/employer.

Don't think you have to find the perfect next job coming out of government service. Look for what interests you, and realize you'll probably change after a couple of years. Understand your values when you start to transition—I valued family and the ability to pick and choose. I didn't want to go to another 50–60 hour a week job working for someone else.

ACKNOWLEDGMENTS

In addition to thanking the 33 Interview Subjects for their contributions to this book, I would like to especially thank Paul Bouwmeester for being a Contributing Author and providing deep subject matter expertise on financial readiness, interview strategies, contract negotiations and corporate benefits. I'd also like to thank him for all his love and encouragement in the long and detailed process of learning how to self-publish a book. There were sleepless nights.

Thanks also to Roger Campbell for being a Beta Content Reviewer of the initial manuscript and providing valuable feedback to make it a better product. I also appreciate the time and efforts of Candi Campbell as an early Beta Content Reviewer and for later reading the revised manuscript a second time as Proofreader. She helped a great deal to polish both the content and the format. I am also grateful to Francis Peck and Kathy Lehmann for their proofreading efforts.

Special thanks go to Carole C. Hayward of Clear Message Media (*www.clearmessagemedia.org*) for her highly professional work in developmental editing and copy editing. Carole also provided very welcome mentoring for this first-time independent author. I would recommend her highly.

I would also like to recognize and recommend long-time friend and Graphic Artist, JoAnn Sullivan (SullivanStudio@comcast.net), for her amazing book cover design and graphics support. Her patience with me has been limitless and greatly appreciated.

Congratulations should also go to Jessica Slater (*www.jslaterdesign.com*) for her highly professional book design and layout work. I recommend her to support your graphics design needs. Her expertise and patience made the book look great!

I am grateful to my brother, Tom Pentz, for providing early proof-reading support. Thanks also to Robert Bouwmeester for his amazing creativity and assistance in marketing support and in website design and e-commerce interface. Appreciation also to Brent Sullivan for providing early graphics support on the pie charts, and to Mark Bouwmeester for technical enabling.

Finally, my deep gratitude to Sue Gordon for her mentorship and support along the way in my career, and especially for sharing her wisdom in the Foreword of this book. She is an inspiration to so many in our special community. I will always treasure our friendship and also our ongoing hoops rivalry. Go, Tar Heels!

All of this is to say thanks, for "it has taken a village" to produce this book. I hope it is useful in your own transition journey.

APPENDIX A

INTERVIEW SUBJECTS' BIOGRAPHIES

Below are the biographies of the 33 Interview Subjects that are quoted throughout the book.

1. Lorie Roule served for 35 years in Intelligence; first at the NSA, then at the CIA in the Directorate of Operations before retiring in 2018. She held several CIA corporate leadership roles, including Chief Talent Development, Executive Lead for Implementation of a Study on Women in Leadership, and Director of CIA's Intelligence Language Institute. She is currently working as a Senior Executive at Transparent Language, Inc., which develops and supports a digital platform for the teaching and learning of languages for U.S. government, schools, libraries, and businesses.

2. Anonymous served as an Operations Officer for more than 20 years in the field of Intelligence. Served in the CIA's Directorate of Operations as a Chief of Station in the field, and as a subject matter expert on

Weapons of Mass Destruction (WMD). She fully retired directly following her government service.

3. Melvin L. Gamble spent 40 years in the field of Intelligence as an Operations Officer with the CIA. He served several tours as a Chief of Station and Deputy Chief of Station. He also served as Deputy Chief of CIA's European Division and Chief of Africa Division. Mel retired in January 2008 and then served as a Vice President for several private sector companies, before starting his own consulting company, Gamble Advisory Group.

4. Vice Admiral Michael LeFever, USN, Retired, served in the United States Navy for 38 years, finishing his military career as the Director of Strategic Operational Planning at the National Counterterrorism Center. Upon leaving government, Mike worked for the McChrystal Group and then IOMAXIS as Chief Operating Officer. Mike currently serves as the Chief Executive Officer for Concentric Advisors, a risk management consultancy. He also is a member of the network of national security experts for "The Cipher Brief".

5. John Sipher spent a 28-year career in the CIA's Directorate of Operations. A member of the CIA's Senior Intelligence Service, John served multiple overseas tours as Chief and Deputy Chief of Station. After leaving government, John worked as a consultant for McChrystal Group and CrossLead. John is a foreign policy and intelligence expert and social media influencer, with articles published in the *New York Times*, *The Atlantic*, *The Washington Post*, *Politico*, *Foreign Affairs*, *Newsweek*, *Slate*, *Lawfare*, and *Just Security*, among others. He regularly appears on the PBS NewsHour, CNN, NPR, MSNBC, BBC and speaks to corporate, academic, and governmental groups. John is currently the co-founder of Spycraft Entertainment, a production firm providing content and talent to the entertainment industry.

6. Anonymous is a retired senior military officer who continues to support the United States Government as a GS employee. Trained as a Foreign Area Officer, this officer spent much of his military career working at the joint and interagency level as a Military Attache' in multiple U.S. embassies, as a staff planner at a combatant command, and in the Pentagon.

7. The Honorable S. Leslie Ireland spent more than 31 years in the Intelligence Community at the CIA, the Treasury Department, and in the Office of the Director of National Intelligence (ODNI). Key assignments included Presidential Daily Briefer for President Obama, DNI Iran Mission Manager, Executive Assistant to DCI Porter Goss and Executive Assistant to DDCIA/Acting DCI John McLaughlin. In her final assignment, she served in a Presidential Appointment as the Assistant Secretary of the Treasury for Intelligence and Analysis and was dual-hatted as the DNI National Intelligence Manager for Threat Finance. Leslie is currently a member of the Board of Directors of Citigroup, Inc., and of The Stimson Center. She is also Chairman of the Financial Threats Council for the Intelligence and National Security Alliance (INSA), and a member of the Cyber Risk Directors Network at Tapestry Networks.

8. Jim Palmucci served 30 years working for the CIA, domestically and abroad, including six years at the National Reconnaissance Office. Jim retired as a Senior Intelligence Officer in 2014 and pursued a second career in the private sector at Accenture Federal Services. Jim continues to provide Financial Coaching services to clients educating them on how to optimize their savings and benefits with the ultimate goal of helping them become financially independent in retirement.

9. Christopher "Chris" Bane served in the U.S. Army. He then joined the CIA as a case officer in the Directorate of Operations. After several tours overseas as a Case Officer and Chief of Station, then as the Deputy Director of an ODNI center, Chris retired after more than 30 years. Chris is now pursuing a second career in the knowledge-driven data analytics industry.

10. William "Bill" French spent his intelligence career leading large, diverse organizations at the CIA and across multiple Intelligence Community agencies, where he specialized in the cyber and technical collection missions. Bill left an indelible legacy in government as an advocate and participant in Employee Resource Groups on diversity efforts.

After 33 years of service, Bill semi-retired to Springfield, MO with his husband, Gary, and their two loving dogs.

11. Ambassador (ret.) Reno Leon Harnish III served 33 years in the U.S. Foreign Service, including Ambassadorial postings abroad. His final assignment (2006-09) in the Department of State was Principal Deputy Assistant Secretary for Oceans, Environment and Science. Following retirement, he worked for eight years as Director of the Center for Environment and National Security at the University of California, San Diego. He is currently retired in the San Diego Area. He has been traveling the world with Leslie Harnish, the love of his life for 52 years.

12. Sheila Flynn served for 34 years in the field of Intelligence as an Operations Officer for the CIA. She spent most of her career overseas, but also developed a passion for intelligence education and developing young talent. Sheila retired in 2017 and now works as an independent consultant for various organizations. Since retirement, Sheila cherishes spending time with family, especially her nephews and nieces, who have grown into amazing young adults. Sheila enjoys spending time at the beach, distance walking, travel, and books.

13. Megan "Mia" McCall served 33 years in the field of Intelligence as an Operations Officer for the CIA. She held several assignments in the foreign and domestic field, including Chief of Station, as well as senior management positions at CIA headquarters. In the latter part of her career, Mia obtained experience at the strategic level serving as Senior Advisor for Foreign Partnerships at ODNI, and in the same capacity in Office of the Deputy Director for Operations Mia retired in 2017 to pursue a second career as a full-time Intelligence and Leadership Educator, obtaining Instructional Systems Design (ISD) certification. Mia is currently providing eldercare support and enjoying the good life in California while teaching part time as an independent contractor.

14. Jerry Powers began his career as a Signals Intelligence professional in the U.S. Navy in 1976, followed by a 30-year career with NSA in analytic and managerial positions. Jerry also had liaison assignments representing NSA at the Office of Naval Intelligence, the Joint Chiefs of Staff, the U.S. Air Force in Europe Headquarters, and two U.S. embassy assignments in Europe. He earned a Master of Science degree in Strategic Intelligence (MSSI) at the Joint Military Intelligence College. Jerry is fully retired and now lives with his wife in Florida enjoying traveling, playing golf, and riding his Harley Davidson.

15. Bonnie Stith worked for the CIA as both Senior Advisor on Cyber to the Director of the CIA, and as Director of the Center for Cyber Intelligence. Bonnie now leads Stith Associates (*stithassociates.com*), working with leaders and organizations to create new success through developing strategic plans that align leadership and culture to organizational mission, vision, and values. Bonnie is an Executive Coach and experienced speaker on cyber threat and response, and on leadership styles and values that create top performing organizational cultures.

16. Karen DeLacy spent a 32-year career as an Operations Officer and senior manager in the CIA's Directorate of Operations (DO). Karen led operations as Chief and Deputy Chief of Station, and headed the DO Leadership and Diversity Training Group. Karen is currently Principal and Founder of DeLacy Associates, providing executive coaching and organizational development consulting in: inclusion and diversity, workplace risk analysis, and international due diligence. She is a certified "Dare to Lead"© Program facilitator.

17. Dolores Powers retired as a Senior Executive from the NSA in 2012 after a 30-year career in a variety of analytic, technical, and managerial positions. Career highlights include three years as the Deputy National Intelligence Officer for the Near East and South Asia on the National Intelligence Council, and three years as a Senior Advisor to the Iran Mission Manager at the ODNI. Dolores fully retired upon leaving government service, and lives seasonally in both Florida and Wisconsin with her husband, Jerry.

18. Jo Ann Moore spent 30 years as a Special Agent with the Department of State's Bureau of Diplomatic Security in positions of increasing responsibility. Noteworthy assignments included: Senior Assistant Regional Security Officer (RSO) U.S. Embassy Baghdad, Chief of Criminal Training Division for the Diplomatic Security Training Center, RSO at the U.S. Mission to the United Nations and U.S. Embassy

Lusaka, Deputy RSO U.S. Embassy Berlin, Assistant RSO U.S. Embassy Tel Aviv, and as Acting RSO to the U.S. Consulate Jerusalem. Since retirement, Jo Ann continues to support RSOs and their offices worldwide on temporary duty assignments as a contractor. Ms. Moore is an avid and passionate tennis player.

19. Deborah B. Christie served for 30 years in the CIA, beginning as a GS-5 clerk typist and ending as a GS-15 Senior Human Resource Chief. During her career, she served in all Agency directorates and traveled overseas to Africa, Central Eurasia, and Europe helping employees with work and personal issues. After deciding up on full retirement, and before her husband passed, they traveled by motorcycle all over the east coast. Debbie was blessed with a job that she loved, great family and friends, but also reminds everyone to balance your personal life and your job, because you never know what the future will bring.

20. Cindy Barkanic served more than 37 years with the CIA as an Economic Analyst on Middle Eastern and North African countries. She was a frequent contributor to the President's Daily Brief and the Economic Intelligence Brief. After leaving government service in early 2020, Cindy founded CSB Coaching Insights. She currently provides career coaching and assessments to help managers at all levels to fine-tune their leadership skills.

21. Mark Post served as an Operations Officer, Deputy Chief of Station, Chief of Station and member of the Senior Intelligence Service during a 26-year career of worldwide assignments in the Directorate of Operations at the CIA. He concluded his government career as the Chief of Operations for a major CIA Mission Center. Following retirement from the CIA, Mark became Vice President of Business Development at Global Guardian, and was subsequently promoted to Chief Operating Officer.

22. Patty Brandmaier retired from the CIA after a 32-year career, the last seven years of which she was a member of the CIA's Senior Intelligence Service. After retiring from the government, Patty worked for the McChrystal Group and later Suntiva. She currently is the Director for Culture, Leadership, and Team Development at Arena Labs, which is pioneering an innovative approach to modern healthcare: High Performance Medicine®.

23. Scott Eder retired from the CIA in 2010 as a career Paramilitary-Operations Officer and member of the Senior Intelligence Service. While at the CIA, Scott had numerous assignments in Africa, the Middle East, and South Asia, as well as multiple positions at Headquarters. Following his retirement from the CIA, Scott worked for Northrop-Grumman for more than two years before starting his own consultant service, which provides support to the Intelligence and Special Operations Force communities. Prior to CIA, Scott served in the U.S. Army Special Forces.

24. Ambassador (ret.) Beth Jones enjoyed a 38-year career in the Foreign Service, achieving the rank of Career Ambassador. She spent most of her career in the Middle East and South Asia, with a mid-career "break" in West Berlin. At the pinnacle of her career, she served as Assistant Secretary of State for Europe and Eurasia. After retirement in 2015, Beth worked in international government relations in the private sector and is now also happily engaged as a pruner in a DC-area landscape company.

25. Maxwell Marker retired after a 23-year career as a Special Agent with the FBI. His career focused mainly on financial fraud and white-collar crime. Assignments included serving as Assistant Special Agent-in-Charge in St. Louis, and several years as a Legal Attaché at a U.S. Embassy abroad. As an FBI Senior Executive, Max served as Chief of the Transnational Organized Crime—Eastern Hemisphere Section prior to his retirement. He now leads a global investigations team focused on internal investigations at Honeywell International.

26. Leslie Harnish retired as a State Department Civil Service Employee in 2019. She had a civil service and non-profit sector career spanning more than 40 years while accompanying her Foreign Service spouse. Leslie worked for the State Department in Rome, Cairo, Stockholm, and in four bureaus in Washington, DC. She credits her most satisfying work in life as the Children's Program Manager for World Vision in Baku, Azerbaijan.

27. Bryan Paarmann - served in the field of National Security for more than 30 years, first as a U.S. Army Officer, and later as a Special Agent and senior leader with the FBI. He held assignments of increasing responsibility both domestically and internationally. Prior to retirement, Bryan was the Special Agent in Charge of the FBI's Counterterrorism Division at their New York Field Office. He also served as the FBI's Deputy Assistant Director for International Operations at FBI Headquarters. Bryan is now Senior Vice President for Security Strategy and Strategic Intelligence at Brosnan Risk Consultants in New York.

28. Terry Roberts served as Director of Requirements and Resources at the Office of the Secretary of Defense, then as the Deputy Director of Naval Intelligence. After transitioning to industry in 2009, Terry became an Executive Director of the Software Engineering Institute at Carnegie Mellon University. She then moved to Total Administrative Services Corporation (TASC) as Vice President of Cyber Engineering and Analytics before founding her own company, WhiteHawk, in 2015. At WhiteHawk, Terry established the first CyberSecurity Online Exchange, enabling businesses to have continuous online access to automated cyber risk profiles, scorecards, action plans, innovative products, services, insights, and trends from across the global cyber risk solution market.

29. Alex Goodale retired from the CIA in 2013 as a Senior Intelligence Service officer after a career in Intelligence spanning more than 41 years, ranging from combat tactical intelligence in Vietnam to Intelligence Community (IC) management. Much of his career focused on technical intelligence, proliferation-related intelligence, and WMD issues. Alex served in multiple IC agencies, including the IC Staff, Defense Intelligence Agency, and Air Force Intelligence. In the years prior to retirement, Alex served as the National Counterproliferation Center's Deputy Director for WMD Security Issues and as the Department of Energy's (DOE) Deputy Director for Intelligence, overseeing the intelligence-related work of DOE National Labs. Alex now works as a consultant on intelligence and national security issues, supporting multiple private- and public-sector clients.

30. Keith Masback served for more than 20 years as a U.S. Army Infantry and Military Intelligence officer, and as a government senior executive on both the Army Staff and at the National Geospatial-Intelligence Agency. After leaving the Federal Government, Keith became CEO of the nonprofit United States Geospatial Intelligence Foundation. Keith is now the Principal Consultant at Plum Run LLC, providing advisory and consulting services to organizations working in geospatial intelligence and related fields.

31. Tresia Gale served for 25 years with the CIA, primarily in the Directorate of Operations (DO). 21 of those years were spent overseas in the Near East and Eastern Europe. Since retiring from government, she has supported the defense-contracting industry and recently became Vice President of Intelligence Programs in a family business venture, Bespoke Technologies, Inc. (BTI), an Economically Disadvantaged Woman-Owned Small Business (EDWOSB).

32. Karen Schaefer served for 26 years at the Central Intelligence (CIA), both as an Operations Officer and senior leader. In addition to working in the Directorate of Operations, she also held senior leadership positions in the Directorate of Science and Technology, the Office of Military Affairs, and served as Executive Assistant to Deputy Director of the CIA. Karen also served as Director of Intelligence Programs at the National Security Council (NSC). She closed out her government career as the Associate Executive Assistant Director of the National Security Branch, Federal Bureau of Investigation (FBI), as the CIA Director's Senior CIA Representative. She currently sits on the Advisory Boards of the International Spy Museum and Third Option Foundation.

33. Anonymous served for more than 25 years in the CIA's Directorate of Operations as an Operations Officer and several-time Chief of Station in the foreign field. She is currently enjoying a second career in the defense contracting industry.

APPENDIX B

AUTHOR BIOGRAPHY
AND BOOK CREDITS

The author, Alison Pentz Bouwmeester, completed a 28-year career as an Operations Officer, Chief of Station and senior leader in the CIA's Directorate of Operations, with frequent geographic moves and job transitions worldwide.

Following her retirement from the CIA, Alison spent nearly a decade as a senior corporate business executive, initially at TASC, where she rose to the level of Vice President for Business Development, and later Agilex Technologies in the same role. Alison subsequently supported corporate efforts in the Intelligence sector at Accenture Federal Services.

In 2018, leveraging 35 years of government and private sector experience, Alison became a Certified Professional Career Coach, and founded

Futurity, LLC to coach others through successful job searches, career advancement, and career transitions.

Alison was inspired to seek a career in government service by her father, Arthur Hollick Pentz, Sr, who left his university studies immediately after the bombing of Pearl Harbor to become a B-17 Pilot during World War II. His plane, "Old Ironsides", was later shot down over Germany and he was held as a Prisoner of War in a German prison camp for 22 months. He remained in the reserves following repatriation, and was later recalled to fly in the Korean War.

Alison and her husband, Paul Bouwmeester, live in Reston, Virginia. They have been married for 30 years, despite the chaos of 7 CIA field tours and two separate, successful professional careers. Alison and Paul continue to enjoy travel, tennis, time with friends and family, and mentoring others. They have two adult sons who are both successfully pursuing their passions as careers.

Alison is a member of the Board of Advisors of the International Spy Museum, and an expert advisor for the Cipher Brief.

APPENDIX C

ADDITIONAL RESOURCES

Get the Lay of the Land:

- *www.washingtonexec.com* and *www.thecipherbrief.com* (Their "Navigating your Transition to Industry" seminar is held several times per year. Get the ground truth from industry representatives on hiring separating Federal Government employees.)

Self-Assessment Tools:

- *www.strengthsfinder.com* (Gallup offers strength assessments to help guide you in your career match.)
- *www.futurityservices.com* (Offering a wide range of assessment resources including: DISC Assessments for Behavioral and

Communication Styles, Motivators and Values, Leadership assessments, Sales IQ assessments, and comprehensive 360s).

- *www.thebalancecareers.com* (Online career assessments and resources)
- *www.careeronestop.org* (Links to assessments and resources by the Dept. Of Labor)
- *www.princetonreview.com/quiz/career-quiz* (Princeton Review's online careers assessment).
- *www.truity.com* (Career and personality assessment)

Professional Development Websites:

- *www.successmagazine.com*

Books:

- *Start with Why* by Simon Simek
- *60 Seconds and You're Hired!* by Robin Ryan
- *Your Executive Image* by Victoria Seitz
- *Take Time for Your Life* by Cheryl Richarson
- *Winning* by Jack Welch
- *Getting Everything You Can Out of All You've Got* by Jay Abraham
- *Do What You Are* by Paul and Barbara Tieger
- *Secrets of Power Conversation* by Lawrence E. Bjornson
- *How to Interview Like a Top MBA* by Dr. Shel Leane
- *Power Interviewing* by Neal Yeager
- *Headhunters Revealed* by Darrell W. Gurney
- *Job Searching Online for Dummies*
- *The New Senior Executive Application* by Diane Hudson
- *Expert Resumé* series by Jist
- *The Career Playbook Essential Advice for Today's Aspiring Young Professional* by James M. Citrin
- *New Passages*, and *Passages for Men* by Gail Sheehy
- *Life's a Bitch, and Then You Change Careers* by Andrea Kay

- *How to write a KILLER LinkedIn Profile* by Brenda Bernstein
- *Your Network is Your Net Worth* by Porter Gale

Career Fairs:

- *www.job-hunt.org*

Job Placement:

- *www.execunet.com*
- *www.recruiterredbook.com/kennedycareerseries*
- *www.kornferry.com*
- *www.bluesteps.com*
- *www.us.manpower.com*

Federal Jobs:

- *www.bradtraverse.com*
- *www.careeronestop.org*
- *www.usajobs.gov*
- *www.myskillsmyfuture.org*
- *www.opm.gov*

Job Boards:

- *www.monster.com*
- *www.career.com*
- *www.indeed.com*
- *www.careerbuilder.com*
- *www.careerexchange.com*
- *www.coolworks.com* (for seasonal work)
- *www.dice.com* (dedicated to engineering and technology jobs)
- *www.job.com*
- *www.jobs.com*

- *www.theladders.com*
- *www.vault.com*
- *www.nationjob.com*
- *www.careersite.com*
- *www.net-temps.com*
- *www.ieee.com* (engineering jobs)
- *www.computerjobs.com* (computer jobs)
- *www.recruitersonline.com*
- *www.headhunter.com*
- *www.jobsingovernment.com* (Federal Government jobs)
- *www.internationaljobs.com* (international jobs)
- *www.intelligencecareers.com*
- *www.usajobs.opm.gov*
- *www.overseasjobs.com*
- *www.workbloom.com* (international jobs)

Job Search Engines:

- *www.careerjet.com*
- *www.indeed.com*
- *www.guardianjobs.com*
- *www.jobseeker.com*
- *www.ceriusconsulting.com*
- *www.employersonline.com*
- *www.entryleveljobs.net*
- *www.hotjobs.com*
- *www.jobster.com*

Military:

- *www.military.com*
- *www.job-hunt.org* (for veterans)
- *www.GIjobs.com*
- *www.milspouse.org/job/jobs/family/*

- *www.military.com/skills-translator?ESRC=careers.nl*
- *www.lockheedmartinjobs.com/military-skills-translator*

Networking:

- *www.linkedin.com*
- *www.xing.com*
- *www.vault.com*
- *www.job-hunt.org/employer_alumni_networking.shtml*
- *www.twitter.com*
- *www.facebook.com*

Recruiters/Headhunters:

- *www.qualigence.com*
- *www.collegerecruiter.com*
- *www.hrmc.com*

Salary Information:

- *www.salary.com*
- *www.glassdoor.com*
- *www.jobstar.org/tools/salary/sal-prof.php*
- *www.datamasters.com*
- *www.mynextmove.org*
- *www.payscale.com*
- *www.jobsmart.org/tools/salary*

Tools to Learn:

- *www.hirevue.com* (video interviewing)
- *www.videobio.com* (desktop video)
- *www.jibberjobber.com*
- *www.skype.com*

- *www.Drive.Google.com*
- *www.Dropbox.com*
- *www.gotomeeting.com*
- *www.adobeconnect.com*
- *www.zoom.us*
- *www.teams.microsoft.com*
- *www.apps.google.com/teams*

Resources for Research on Prospective Employers:

- *www.glassdoor.com*
- *www.businesswire.com*
- *www.corporateinformation.com*
- *www.business.com*
- *www.infospace.com*
- *www.fortune.com*
- *www.ceoupdate.com*
- *www.acinet.org*
- *www.annualreportservice.com*
- *www.corporateinformation.com*
- *www.business.com*
- *www.forbes.com/lists/*
- *www.careers.wsj.com*
- *www.sec.gov* (EDGAR database of SEC filings)
- *www.jobhuntersbible.com*
- *www.ceoexpress.com*
- *www.profileresearch.com*
- *www.vault.com*
- *www.bizjournals.com/bookoflists*

Resources for Scrubbing Your Online Profiles:

- *www.reputationdefender.com*